Choose only Love

The Divine Relationship

BOOK VI

Messages from A Choir of Angels
Received by Sebastián Blaksley

TAKE HEART PUBLICATIONS

ELIGE SOLO EL AMOR | CHOOSE ONLY LOVE

Publication in English authorized by
Fundación amor vivo, a nonprofit organization, Argentina
Av. Libertador 16434
San Isidro
Buenos Aires, Argentina
www.fundacionamorvivo.org

TAKE HEART PUBLICATIONS
13315 Buttermilk Bend
North San Juan, CA 95960
www.takeheartpublications.com
ISBN 978-1-58469-689-6
Cover and editorial design by Alejandro Arrojo
Computer production by
Patty Arnold, *Menagerie Design and Publishing*
Manufactured in the United States of America

Choose only Love

The Divine Relationship

Table of contents

A Message from Sebastián

These messages are for everyone and for all times, in spite of the limitation of human words, which can separate. Love includes everything we are. It takes us beyond our ideologies, cultures, educations, personalities, and beliefs, towards what cannot be expressed in words because love is beyond all limits. But to reach us effectively, the angels express their universal love using concrete symbols—in this case, words. We each come out of a particular cultural context. I am a lay person living in the 21st century, born in Argentina, with a Catholic education, and am very devoted to my faith. Therefore the flavor of these messages reflects my Catholic orientation; however, I clearly understood that love is universal and addressed to everyone and everything. Love is always inclusive.

As Jesus says in Book 5 of this series:

It is important that you remember that names, like words, have no meaning of their own in relation to the realm of divine truth. Do not forget that love has no words. However, in the plane of perceptions, names, like words, can mean a lot. Names that are used, such as Jesus, Mary, Holy Spirit, and God, have been endowed with many meanings over the centuries. We cannot escape the laws of perception while living in the world; nor is there any reason to do so. The love of God does not overlook anything in your world, but rather joins with it, and from that union, transforms it, together with you, so that the truth that is beyond every word shines freely.

I hope with all my heart that you feel included in the embrace of God's love through these messages from Heaven. But merely reading them will not bring you to Heaven's gate; rather, they are a port of departure or springboard from which you are encouraged daily to express with your particular voice the Divine Love that lives in you—increasingly to make known that part of love that only you can manifest.

If you are able to understand the words and symbols of this work as a means and not as an end, and receive these messages primarily with the heart rather than the thinking mind, you will go beyond the symbols towards the love that they evoke. You will begin to remember your first love, that is, for God. These writings are a love letter from God the Father/Mother to His/Her beloved daughters and sons. It is directed to the healing of memory so that, once healed, the remembered love that has no beginning or end shines in you.

I. How It Originated

On October 3, 2018, a presence that was all love and whose magnificence, beauty, and benevolence cannot be described, came to me suddenly in a way I had never before experienced. I understood with perfect clarity that it was the glorious Archangel Raphael. He introduced himself saying, "I am the medicine of God." He told me to pray a particular prayer for nine days. Through inner inspiration he also dictated certain intentions for me to pray. The prayers consisted of five Our Fathers, five Hail Marys, and five Glories, just as these prayers are presented in the Catholic Church, to which I belong.

On October 13, the day after finishing this novena of prayer, I began to receive glorious visits from a choir of countless angels of God accompanied by Archangel Raphael and Archangel Gabriel. Their love and beauty were indescribable. Through the choir came the Voice of Christ, expressed in an ineffable form and as images, shown in symbols visible to the spirit. I put the meaning of these images into written words, then into voice recordings.

Each visitation was the same: First I received the images and heard the music that the choir presents, then the chorus departed while Archangels Raphael and Gabriel remained as custodians, or loving presences, until the message or session in question was transcribed.

The glorious Archangel Raphael is the one who guides me in the transcription, assuring that the message is properly received and that what is shown can be passed from image to word. Archangel Gabriel is the loving custodian of everything that concerns the work, not only in reference to the manifestation itself and to the writings, but to everything that arises and will arise from them.

The messages, or sessions, are shown to me as a picture of great beauty in which each form (which has no form) is in itself a voice, a "sound-image." What I hear is like the rhythmical twanging of a harp that becomes translated into words. This tune is a vibration of celestial music whose frequency is unlike the sounds of the world. It is a kind of "vibration-frequency" that the soul knows perfectly well and that I recognize with certainty as the voice of the Lamb of God. Once everything is transcribed in written and spoken words, then the chorus arrives in all its glory once again, as if they were coming to seek the most holy Archangels Raphael and Gabriel. Then all together they retire, singing a hosanna to the Christ of God.

That hosanna sung by the choir of angels is a majestic song of praise and gratitude to the Creator for the infinite mystery of love that is the Second Coming. It is a prelude to His coming. If humankind were able to understand in all its magnitude the ineffable mystery of love that is the Second Coming of Christ, we would eternally sing the mercies of God in union with all the angels.

In cases where the Virgin Mary Herself or Jesus Christ are present in their human and divine person and communicate directly, the choir of angels is muted with love, in a silence that is sacred. Pure expectation, so to speak, surrounds their blessed presences. The angels bow their heads, cast their eyes downward, and are caught up in an ecstasy of love, veneration, and contemplation. Nothing and no one dares, nor could, interrupt the holy silence in which the universe is submerged before the sovereign presence of Mary and Jesus when they speak directly to our souls. This is because that space of dialogue between Christ and the soul is inviolable. It is the sacred temple of the intimacy of the soul with God.

When Archangel Raphael makes himself present to me and begins the process of translating images and symbols into written words, my will is fused into one will with him. We are one and the same will. There is no "you" and "me." And yet, even in that unity, there is the consciousness that I am I, and he is he: two persons with the same will, the same consciousness of being, in a single holy purpose. My thinking mind is silenced in this absorption of my being into the being of all true being, which we share as a unit. My consciousness and his become one. What the will of one says to be done, is done. There is no distance between the "be done" and its effect.

The rest of my humanity responds humbly. There is no resistance. There is only a flow of words coming from the Mind of Christ, as if it were from a spring that flows from the top of a mountain. This torrent of Grace made into words makes my fingers fly with speed and precision that far surpasses that of my ordinary writing. The soul remains ecstatic with love and with a single desire—to remain forever fused with the beloved Christ, being of our being and of all true being.

During the visitations my whole being is bathed in great peace and joy, like being embraced by universal love. But after concentrating on putting the message into words, the body shows great fatigue. It seems that it is difficult for it to sustain the energy I receive. The part of the manifestation that includes the chorus of angels, the voice, and the images is something that can happen at any time, place, or in any circumstance. However, the transcription of the symbols received into written words and then spoken and recorded can be delayed until I can make myself available to do so. It may be immediately afterwards or several days later.

The main message of this work could be summarized as follows: The time for a new humanity has arrived, a humanity that is ready to manifest the living Christ in each of us. We are, each of us, Christ. This is the truth about us, even if we perceive ourselves differently. We are already prepared to be able to live life in the certainty that says: I no longer live, but it is Christ who lives in me. Helping us to realize this truth in our lives, here and now, is what this manifestation is about. All of Heaven will help us in this holy purpose, since it is the Second Advent itself.

II. A Description of the Manifestations

When the Archangels come, they come without wings. They are like humans wearing tunics. Raphael's tunic is green, edged with gold. Gabriel's tunic is pink, almost white, edged with yellow. Both tunics are majestic, appearing as if made of a very precious silk.

Their faces are cheerful and radiant, with very light yellowish skin. Both have shoulder-length, golden blond hair and their eyes are green. They each have unique facial features. Their bodies are ra-diant with serene glowing light that generates peace and a great sense of beauty and harmony.

Many of the angels in the Chorus of Angels have light pink and light blue tunics. Others have light gold, but all are pastel colors, again with a serene luminosity. A few have green robes as if they were emeralds but a little lighter.

The permanent happiness that angels exhibit is remarkable. Everything is joy with them. One day they told me that they radiate perpetual happiness because they always share happiness.

The angels are always surrounded by white and majestic light, as if they live in an eternal mid-day of love and light. They are accompanied by music, as though a celestial choir is singing in all cor-ners of the universe, like the sound of millions of harps playing in unison, forming a harmonious symphony of great beauty.

The angelic vibrations are of such a degree that they calm the mind and the heart, and give peace. One knows, without knowing how, that this vibration is simultaneously prayer and praise. Each part of the universe (creation) sings a song of gratitude for it having been called into existence, as though it has music inside that is a prayer to the Creator. The human soul had stopped hearing this ce-lestial music but will begin to hear it again when it returns to the Father's house. Though forgotten, this song is forever loved by souls that love the Father and Creator.

The ineffable, inexpressible beauty of these visions of angels and archangels submerges the soul in an ecstasy of love and rapture in which one's whole being participates. No joy or happiness on Earth compares with the ecstasy that a vision of the greatness, magnanimity, and beauty of the angels and arch-angels generates.

Angelic intelligence is of such a degree that it surpasses all worldly understanding. Their thoughts occur at an indescrib-able speed, even faster than human thought. Without distortion of any kind, their thoughts are pure, without contradiction, with perfect clarity, and express only holiness. As lightning crosses the firmament, so too do angelic thoughts pass through my mind.

I clearly perceive the difference between human thought and thought from the Wisdom of Heaven, due to the way I experience each. Thoughts from Heaven feel like light and breath; they are full of certainty, can never be forgotten, and they bring a great "amount" of truth in the blink of an eye. In an instant I understand the full meaning of each manifestation that comes to me.

Humility, prudence, and simplicity are central features of the angels. Their greatest joy is to serve God by being servants of all creation. They love human beings, animals, plants, stones, the ele-ments, and every material and immaterial aspect of creation with a love and tenderness that, when ex-perienced, is capable of melting even the hardest heart.

While the beauty and magnanimity of angelic visions are indescribable, they are a pale flash compared to the magnif-icence of those of Jesus and Mary. Nothing in the universe resembles the eter-nal, unnamable beauty of the hearts of Jesus and Mary. They are God made man and woman. They are the joy of the angels and have the veneration of creation. From them springs all harmony, greatness, and holiness.

The looks of Jesus and Mary, radiating such tenderness and love, melt the entire universe. Their smiles are purity itself. In their presence the soul is entranced in an ecstasy of venera-tion and contemplation, leaving it speechless. The soul exhales a moan of joy that says something like Ah! For me personally, contemplating the looks and smiles of Jesus and Mary is Heaven.

I hope you can understand what I'm trying to say as I try to describe the indescribable. I only say what I see, hear, and expe-rience. Heaven exists, God exists, and God is love. This is what was giv-en to me to see, hear, and understand.

I hope with all my heart that those who receive this manifestation let themselves be the beloved of God, more and more every day; and in this way be transformed by the beauty of a love that has no beginning nor end.

With love in Christ,

Sebastián Blaksley,
A Soul in Love
Buenos Aires, Argentina
January, 2019 and October, 2020

Prelude

*A song expressed by the voice of the beloved for his beloved,
the voice of Christ for a soul in love.*

Blessed soul of the Father, sweetness of my divine and loving heart! Beauty of creation! How sweet is your look! How great your purity!

Tell me, enlightened soul, delight of my being,
Where does the wind go when it blows? What makes it move?
Where do tulips come from?
Who makes the birds of the air sing?
Where is light born?
Who has given beauty to the sun?
Where does love dwell?

Daughter of wind and light, beloved of God, my heart sings jubilantly to be with you. United we are the light of the world. In our love lies the source of life, because I created everything for you. Eve-rything belongs to you because everything is mine.

I gave <u>you</u> life. I gave you a heart. I gave you the beauty of the seas. I created light and stars for your joy. I did everything for you. Everything your eyes see and beyond is a sacred gift of my love for you—a flash of my holy being for my beloved.

How beautiful is our love story! How eternal and how unfin-ished. No one can ever write it, be-cause what happens within the sacred precinct of our union cannot be seen nor heard by anything or anyone except you and me.

Oh, divine intimacy of a soul in love, source of perfect creation, origin of life!

Oh, holy love, divine relationship! From you all light arises, each fountain springs from your bosom. The birds fly toward you. The whole universe is heading toward you. From you come the waters of dew that surround the Earth and return to you.

Oh, divine union! Who can express your beauty? Who, your wisdom? You are the source of life, the reason for existence.

Oh, divine relationship, residence of love, House of Truth, Kingdom of Heaven! In you angels rejoice and souls together sing a song of perfect love.

Blessed are you who have come here, for you have entered into the dwelling place of God.

1.

The Unknown Saints

A message from Archangel Raphael

I. Gratitude and Freedom

Beloved child, this is a holy encounter between Heaven and Earth. Here we are united with you and with everything beautiful, real, and sacred. We have come clad in light, with spread wings of freedom. We do it through this expression of pure love and divine truth that together we create for the love of humanity and God.

We come in the eternity that we are. We come from all places and from all times because we belong to the divine sphere which encompasses everything.

We are both a multitude and singularities. We are your soul friends forever and ever. In the Heaven of your holy mind, in the paradise of your heart, resides the awareness of what God is, and with it the Kingdom where wisdom dwells.

What you have in the Kingdom is part of your being; therefore what you are and what you have are one and the same. That is why you have been told time and again that you are Heaven. Its reality is seen by the Christ consciousness which gives it existence, in the sense that it makes it known to itself. Remember that consciousness is what makes being aware of its own reality, making it known to itself.

A new light shines on the Earth. A new song is sung in Heaven. This song of holy love resounds in every corner of the universe. Birds sing. Waters dance. Pure hearts rejoice. A new love has been born from our union.

Beloved of the angels of Heaven! Purity of God made humanity! We, your brothers and sisters created to serve the Most High, love you with an angelic love, a love without beginning nor end, the love of the Holy Trinity.

We are the flame of living love and desire that you be lit with the holy fire of the knowledge of God that burns in us. We join your light; and thus united, we merge into a new luminescence whose brilliance comes from the source of all light, just as the faint glow of the moon reflects the sun.

Oh, my beloved! Beloved of all that is true! Living miracle of the Creator! The mere idea of us existing without you is impossible. We know, because our hearts know, that Heaven would not be Heaven without your presence. If you had not made the choice for love, creation would have been colored with a hue that Mother God did not create, that is not part of Her palette of holy colors.

How much I love you, light of my eyes, holy beauty! Our whole being shudders at your presence because in you lives our beloved Christ. To God is all power, all glory and all praise. To Her, all honor.

Know that you are a temple of wisdom, a house of prayer, a mountain of contemplation. You are the ivory tower where all that God created for you inhabits, without anything that could desecrate it. You are beautiful. You are a blessing.

What a joy it is to walk this path of love and truth with you. Let us thank the Father-Mother whose will has arranged for this holy voice to be expressed on Earth through these words. You, like all creation, need the living word, presented and expressed in various ways over time. That is why our Creator continues to communicate the word of eternal life.

I am Archangel Raphael. I have been correctly called the Medicine of God. I am that, because I am love and love heals all ailments. I am a living expression of the holy love of the Father. I am he who day and night watches over you, even if you do not feel me nor hear me with the ears of your spirit nor see me with the eyes of your soul. For love I wrap you warmly during winter nights when cold hearts try, even without realizing, to put out the fire of divine relationship.

Throughout this work we have spoken often of the mind, the heart, and the reality of the Divine Mind that lives in you and in the Sacred Heart of Jesus who, together with the Immaculate Heart of Mary, form a Holy Trinity with your heart. In this new light you have known yourself.

We have traveled a path full of blessings, beginning with the path of the heart. Then, always united to the unconditional love of God who gave us eternal forgiveness, we moved to the path of transformation, thanks to which you have become a new divine being.

Transformed into a divinized being, you plunged into the unfathomable abyss of the path of knowledge, a path that, through the light of holiness, led to the blessed memory of who you are.

After having reached that holy abode, after touring the serene river of perfect knowledge, your being met the wisdom of love, the only wisdom necessary and possible. In it you attained superior knowledge. You understood that everything is relationship.

With that sacred understanding we begin now to walk together on new paths.

We thank the roads traveled for everything they have given us. We bless the past and all history, ours and that of all human-kind. We honor the paths of life and leave them behind.

We turn our heads gently and with the sanctity of our eyes, look upon everything we have lived, the love received, and the miracle of life. We are left alone for a single moment, contem-plating this vision. And then we say goodbye forever to what we see, and with a smile say in the silence of the heart:

"Thank you Father-Mother God for giving me life. Thank you for being as you are: pure mercy, pure compassion. Thank you, each path of my life, for bringing me here where I can dwell forever in the sweetness of love. I leave you with my blessing as I continue now on this new path at whose doors I find myself. You have left me here and cannot come with me. I bless you in the name of love."

After having blessed everything lived, known, taught, and experienced, we let it go forever and begin a new path, a path without past, without plans, without pre-conceived ideas. We are carried by the Grace of God.

II. Mystery and Relationship

There has been talk of the relationship you have with everything—with your mind, with your heart, with who you are, with your feelings and thoughts, with God and with others. The beauty of holy relationship and the unitive rela-tionship with Christ, the only real relationship, has been clearly and beautifully expressed.

Now we take another step. We will stretch our minds toward what has never been said, seen, or heard, but which the heart knows. We enter the infinite chasm of the divine relationship.

Just as ego-based relationships, or special relationships, had to be seen for what they were before we could move towards holy relationship, we dare now to commit to be bold.

Your humanity will be completely absorbed in that which is beyond all human thought, while remaining what it is. Humanity and divinity will now embrace, establishing a new bond of love linking the Supreme Source with the nature of the human. And with that we will become increasingly aware of a union that is above all union, and includes them all.

Beloved mirror of wisdom! What a joy it is to be able to sing with you a new song every morning, every sunset, and every night!

What joy our pure souls feel, united with yours, to be able to create eternally new universes of infinite love, universes that live in our pure hearts!

We are the reality of perfect charity. We are the glory of the Father of Lights, manifested in a way that makes the heart dance and the mind rest in the sweet arms of love.

Who can say what the soul experiences in a divine relationship? None can. And yet we will do so in this unique work, full of angelic love, holy love, full of seraphic wisdom and celestial beauty.

What will be said in this sixth book will be unique, because there are no two identical expressions of what is created in the divine relationship between the soul and its sacred source. Nevertheless, the loving hearts that have made the choice for love will know how to drink from the source of wisdom that this work offers. And so, like cymbals that resonate with grace and harmony, their souls will vibrate to the beat of eternal truth.

They will join the choir of angels that this manifestation gives. They will sing with us a song of love that lasts forever.

You, who are of the truth, will recognize who it is now speaking to your heart. Through these words you will hear God on Earth. And you will be happy in the memory of your first love which you have already found, and into which you melt more each day.

Beloved pure soul! You who live for God! Whoever joins this work becomes one with us, and because of that union miracles and spiritual events of incalculable greatness and bliss will occur. Gates of Heaven not yet opened will do so.

These writings are a conduit through which the Grace of God will flow to countless numbers of sisters and brothers, including those who are in time, those who have already left, and those who will come to choose again. These words will be like a footprint that others will follow with certainty to take them without delay or detour to the holy abode. All of them, in union with you, with me, and with Heaven, will be embraced by the love of Jesus and Mary. Together we will live forever in the reality of love. Together we will sing victoriously the song of eternal life.

Choosing only love is that for which you have come to this universe. Nothing else. Showing the way for others to make this choice consciously is the highest form of sharing because it is the way to share God.

To choose only love is to choose only God. It is to remain only in the Kingdom, and allow the rest to be added unto you.

Brother, sister, you have come to choose again, and you have chosen. What joy! What greater joy can there be than to fulfill the purpose of Heaven?

Oh, divine child! Let these words enter your heart. Let a love song be sung to you. Imbibe the sweetness of Christ. Rest in the truth.

The only obstacle to enlightenment, to supreme knowledge, is fear. Often a soul undertakes long processions, fasts, meditations, exercises of all kinds, reading books or practicing devotions. All will finally pay off if you are grounded in sincerity of heart, not because of the acts or renunciations performed, but because of your holy purpose of knowing God.

The merit of spiritual "doing" resides solely in the awareness of your desire to live in the truth, your desire to live in the Mother's house, your longing for perfect love. Such desire is not minor but very important.

But fear overrides your awareness of love. Fear makes you lose sight of love. Therefore, I say with certainty that although you may do many things to reach God, if you are unwilling to put aside fear, none of what you may spiritually "do" will help you, but rather it will bolster your ego.

I have called this session "the unknown saints." It might also have been called "the enlightened strangers." What I want to express is that many kinds of beings have attained enlightenment, that is, higher knowledge or the wisdom of love. Their common denominator is that they have chosen love as the center and the reason for life. They have chosen truth as their eternal companion no matter where they are or what they do. They live consciously for God and in God, even though the totality of the effects of their choice are not completely known while they remain functioning on Earth.

They know that supreme knowledge is eternal, even beyond the physical plane, while continuing to provide a service to their sisters and brothers to love with ever greater degrees of understanding of love and union with Christ. In that understanding of the inescapable sufficiency of truth, they rest in peace, amazed and eternally surprised by the greatness of the wisdom of love. What they know ceases to be perceived as a lack, and is understood as what it is, a constant knowing of God, constantly growing as a more beautiful, serene, and holy knowledge. Put simply, they become fully aware of the infinity of truth.

III. Contrasts in the Light

The millions of sisters and brothers who throughout the world are living their human lives being the enlightened ones of God, those who found love, embody all varieties of social, religious, philosophical, moral, and other characteristics. Almost none are well known, because to be a celebrated saint is simply one option among several. Few choose that path, nor is it necessary. Indeed, there are few; otherwise they would not be famous.

There is a relationship between the known saints and the strangers of the world, one that makes the other what it is. If all the enlightened ones were notorious and their works spectacular for the curiosity of humanity to be encouraged, then the spiritual life, as a path and option, would cease to be attractive to beginners.

The curiosity of the ego is one of the main means the Holy Spirit uses in favor of the truth among the children of God as they begin the path of glory. You have an expression that explains what I am saying here: a little bit pleases but much angers. In other words, what is scarce has more value than that which is abundant, a fact upon which your whole economic system is based. That concept is deeply ingrained in the human mind, so the spirit of wisdom uses that belief and applies it as an incentive towards spiritual search.

The spiritual path almost always begins with curiosity. If all the saints were constantly known instead of remaining hidden to human eyes—although always visible in the eyes of God—

then your curiosity would not prompt you to undertake the fascinating path of the search for being. Can you begin to see this? When we described the way of Mary and the way of Jesus, we also tried to describe this truth.

As far as you are concerned we only care that you be aware that there are those on the spiritual path who have notoriety, as well as others who are unknown. Both are equally holy, equally servants.

Both options have the same effect on humanity and the universe as a whole because your choice was not an option made in time, but in eternity. It was for Heaven and not for the perishable, just as the sun's rays embrace the smallest blades of grass, born from a much higher place that gives life to everything.

Remember, love is not something you can search for and find. Love is what you are. With this re-affirmation, we avoid falling into the error of believing that you are on the right track if you are followed by multitudes of sisters and brothers, or if you write wonderful books that are read by many. That small handful of beings touched by you are but a tiny bit of sand compared to the vast number of beings that your true love embraces, transforms, and sanctifies. Remember that in the end, in the realm of the eternal, there is no notion of quantity, size, or degree.

When it was said that "he who is holy in little ways is great," we sought not only to give a guide to behavior and discernment, but to convey the truth that it is not necessary to do great things, but small things with great love.

Every human work is itself but a tiny daisy petal to the entire universe; yet since the essence of life is love, if that action has the effect of love, then it carries within itself all the power of Heaven and Earth regardless of how visible it may be in the eyes of the world.

Beloved child! God, who sees in secret, knows the greatness of your love. Christ, who loves simplicity, knows the beauty of your works born of your unconditional love for him. Mary, who gave you new life, is fully aware of the purity of your heart and knows very well that all the power of the glory of Heaven flows through your being as an inevitable result of who you are.

Those who live in the truth know that their light does not come from them; they rejoice being the extension of the Father-Mother God. They know they are relative, not absolute beings. They do not seek to occupy the place that only belongs to God, just as the child would not think of taking the place that only belongs to the parent. Both live in the truth of what they are. They are sincere. They are honest with themselves, and therefore with everyone and everything.

They know that although fear is able to overshadow love in a singular consciousness, it cannot tear it out. Thus they do everything in their power to put aside fear and live forever in love.

Those who have chosen love know what it means to live in the truth and are glad to remain in it every day. They do not give different names to what is the same. They do not seek to change reality. They only love because they are love.

They illuminate with their silence or their noisy presence. They know that God is not philosophy, science, theology, nor poetry. They know that God is love and that they are one with God. They are one with love. They are the light of the world. They know the mysteries of life because they know who they are. They know true wisdom because they have recognized love. On that knowledge they base their existence. On that knowledge they live in the light of truth.

Hear me, all! Those who come to this work will be my beloved saints unknown to the world, but known forever in my love.

There are as many paths to the truth as there are minds and hearts. Even so, this work proposes one path in particular, a path to which all others lead.

You can reach it through asceticism, devotion, sacrifice, relaxation, renunciation of effort, intellect, meditation, prayer, or any other means. You can come here having literally separated yourself from the environment in which you lived, or through spiritual reading, dance, expressions of art, or having dedicated your life to religious activity. Or without any of those things.

Philosophy can take you to the door of the path offered here, and sometimes also science and theology. But none of them, including devotion and action, can go beyond the point of entry.

Remember, love is not something you have to think about, nor put into words, nor is it something you do. Love is what you are. Therefore, the supreme knowledge consists in knowing what you really are. This cannot be repeated too often, given its capital importance.

In true knowledge, which comes from knowing your being in the light of eternal truth, you know the divine relationship. The path proposed in this work is the path of being. This path travels within the divine relationship, the direct relationship with God. On this path—in the awareness of the relationship between your being and your source and what the purpose and reality of divine relationship means—is the achievement of wisdom.

As was said before, to seek a direct relationship with God is to seek wisdom, knowledge, and truth. Therefore it is not necessary to spend hours, days, or years sitting under a tree, or to be nailed to a cross, or to travel the world to share a wisdom that doubtless is worthy of being shared. Nor is it necessary for you to prophesize, predict the future, or release oppressed peoples.

It is not necessary to attract congregations or create communities of divine knowledge. True knowledge proceeds from—and is—the divine relationship, and is only achieved in it. Its form of expression is individual, but wisdom itself is universal.

To return to the direct relationship with God is to return to truth, or, put another way, is to choose love. This is the only choice that human beings need to make. The physical world is not a place to pay for sins whether committed in the immediate or ancestral past. There is no such thing as a law of karma. There is no karma in the children of God, only consciousness becoming aware of what it really is.

Your being is, in its relation to God, a relative and not absolute being, in which knowing yourself is knowing yourself in relation to God, in relation to the sacred source of life, in relation to your holy origin, in relation to love.

When you can look upon all things and events from the relationship that everything has with love and that love has with everything, you will have fulfilled your divine purpose. Indeed, you will have fulfilled the only true purpose that can be fulfilled.

2.

The Art of Living

A message from Jesus, identifying himself as "the living Christ who lives in you"

I. Prelude

My love! Purity created by love! What a joy it is for us to be alone with you, to write from Heaven and receive the wisdom of love. We must also love you in your freedom, and so we respect your time and the tasks of the world. Our relationship will never be an interference in your life, but it will be the essence of your reality. We are in union. We are with you at all times and places. Not only do we help to write this work, we also help you receive what Christ consciousness has determined to be received by you through this blessed work and in every other holy moment.

We are with you when you sleep, when you prepare breakfast, when you dive into prayer. We are one with you even when you are doing worldly things, whatever they may be. Remember that you are alive but it is Christ who lives in you.

A bright and splendid light surrounds you everywhere, though the body's eyes see it not. The beauty of your light extends to the ends of the universe, giving light and life to everything. It is the light of the living Christ shining in you. It is the light of your being.

Wrapped in the halo of holiness in which you were created, you dissipate the fog, causing the clouds to transform into rain and return to Earth the water that was removed through the condensation of consciousness.

Oh, holy child of God! Soul that lives eternally! Oh, pure holy soul! Blessing of creation! You who have made the choice for love and have become aware of the divine relationship in which you exist and are, remember that a spring of thanks and miracles flows from the heart of the Mother of the living towards your being and from you to everything that exists. Blessed soul, you are the light of the world and your function is to illuminate. This fact is so powerful that even though we explain it in a thousand different ways, we will never be able to embrace the inescapable mystery of love and truth that you are.

You are my sun, and illumination is the sun's function. You are a child of light. You are a child of the wind. You are a child of God: light, wind, and love; or power, movement, and creation. These are the three pillars of being.

This sixth book of this work from Heaven, given to the world through my loving and generous scribe, focuses on the final preparation for your eternal ministry—your mission or work for the love that God is. Accordingly we dedicate time to unravel the mystery of light, or enlightenment.

When you have finished this book, and even more when you have completed this work in its entirety, you will have no doubt about your purpose in the universe and in the world.

I make a distinction between "universe" and "world" so that you remember that there are infinite realities to create and that have already been created within the pure potential of the divine being. When I refer to "world," I refer to your constellation of relationships as an individual and collectively, with everything that is part of the physical plane. That is your "world." Remember that it has countless dimensions. Creation has no limit.

It is necessary to clarify this definition of "world" and to remember it, given the confusion that has occurred since I stepped onto the Earth and taught. I spoke of the reality of "the world" and "the Kingdom of Heaven" as opposite realities. I will discuss this here.

You did not create the universe. You did not create the world either. But you did create and constantly create your "world." It is that world I have been speaking of for a very long time. Your "world" is a concept that approaches truth in the sense that it expresses what happens in your mind and heart, and within it, how you relate to everything. Thus you create your inner and outer "world."

In a sense, the word "world" seeks to define the relationship you have with everything. And since that relationship is determined by the relationship you have with who you are, and in turn directly linked to the relationship you have with God, the source of your being, then the divine relationship is everything.

During the course of this Heavenly manifestation that God has wanted to give to humanity, a work which is unique and perfect because of its purpose, we have been exploring the reality of the soul's relationship with the Creator, of your being with God. This is how we started when we began to walk together along this path so full of wisdom and truth. We will continue for all eternity. Being aware of this is the essence of enlightenment and knowledge.

II. Light, Wind, and Love

Within the framework of this work, enlightenment means to embody the living Christ who lives in you. To embody love. This is because God only relates to Her one child, that is, Christ. This matter of the "only begotten son of God" has also created some confusion. I will not expand on it, but will say the following.

God has only one child. That child is Her divine being. In reality, all relate only to their being, and from that relationship all other relationships arise. Truly I tell you that God and you have only one child, your being, just like me and every living being.

God's Being we call Christ, love, child of God, or Kingdom of Heaven. Since that is the only true, real being, when you were created, you were given Christ to be what you are. In other words, the Creator of your being could not give you another being than Her own, since there can be nothing alien to the being that She is. This is the same as saying that love gives of itself because it has nothing else to give, since there is nothing outside of itself. Whether or not you accept this truth is something else entirely, but reason will tell you that it is true. There can be no true being other than the being that God is.

You can be the child of God on Earth and in Heaven because you can be your true being, completing your path to the truth by walking in truth.

So that you do not get lost in abstraction, and for this to be clearly understood, it is important that you remember, beloved child, that every path of life that each of you has is in itself a path of enlightenment, of truth. It is in itself a path to supreme knowledge. If you open yourself in your mind and heart you can reach the fullness of love. There is no reason not to do so except for the conscious, free, and deliberate decision not to do so, which is to embrace fear rather than the joy of love.

True knowledge and enlightenment are the same. It is not reached by effort or action but exclusively by divine revelation. It is a gift. Just as life was given you, love was also given you. Where it makes an appearance you may recognize love as a gift from the Creator. But it is also true that you can prepare to receive it, and that your disposition is valuable, a pure present to your Father-Mother God and Creator, although even your disposition or renunciation are not required conditions.

You can incarnate Christ without mental activity. You can embody love without the ability to speak, or even the ability to express anything with the body. Moreover, you can incarnate Christ without even being a human being. Plants can embody the living Christ, as can animals and the elements of matter. In short, being the embodiment of love is possible for all who inhabit Earth, and for the physical universe as a whole.

Do not worry about whether you meditate or not, whether you read the right books or not, or even if you act rightly. Only and exclusively take care to keep your mind and heart open to receive love. As long as you receive the love of God, you will become one with Him. The rest is a matter of the unity of your being with its sacred source, that is, of your direct relationship with God.

You—yes, you—must reach and remain in Divine Love. It is what you are here and now. Embrace all of it, accept what you are being in every moment, how you gather within your heart what you are. With this, you live in unity and allow your being to become aware of the divine relationship, your relationship with God.

The relationship of Divine Love is not one in which two separate beings look at each other at a distance, much less as if they were related by indifference or violence. It is a relationship of pure love, of unity, a link in which what you are and your source become one, like the lover and loved one who by joining can no longer be happy without each other. Or like a loving mother and her newborn. Or like a grateful father whose light is his son.

Remember, it is on Earth that you begin to recognize love. Those who say they love God, whom they do not see, but do not love their brother who they do see, live in illusion. It is necessary to begin to love what is seen in order to finally be able to love what cannot be seen.

The path of life that each of you are traveling is the path of awakening to love. It is the perfect path for awakening to occur.

It is true that some wake up sooner, others later. But it is important to recognize, in the serene light of truth, that from the moment you are born into the world you begin to awaken to the consciousness of love. You become more aware of who you are, and that what you are is love, and then you awaken to the love you really are. Each of you is waking up to the truth that you are, regardless of the form that each of your lives takes.

The state of unconsciousness—or more accurately stated, of denial of love or the deep sleep of Adam—is prior to your incarnation on the physical plane. When you entered the dimension of space and time, you began, so to speak, the last phase of the awakening of consciousness.

This has also been discussed, although I do it now from a new perspective. I do it in the recognition that none are more awakened or less enlightened, more awake or less awake. Either you live in the light or you live in darkness. Either you are awake or you are asleep.

Everyone in the world has woken up. That was necessary for them in order to make the choice they have made. No one can truly choose while asleep, except to continue to sleep or to wake up. That choice is not made in this world, but prior to entering it.

The choice that all are called to make is the choice for love. For this you must reach a degree of consciousness that allows you to make this choice. The dimensions of time, space, and matter collaborate.

For this you have come to the world: to choose again. Even so, once you awaken, you have to travel a path. Life is movement.

Let us put this together. The life you live in this world takes you from a state of unconsciousness to that of full awareness of the truth of who you are. This path has its sequential phases.

The stages of awakening can be described as follows. One begins on the path of the heart. Next you begin the path of transformation. When transformed, you travel the path of knowledge. As soon as you reach the supreme knowledge and choose to live in the truth that has been revealed to you through wisdom that is not of the world, then, and only then, do you begin to walk the only eternal path, the way of being.

These paths, concatenated with each other, begin to be traveled with greater or lesser degrees of consciousness, but all have a common denominator: forgiveness and love, which are like the two legs with which the soul walks. These legs are no longer needed when you complete the path of knowledge. On the path of being you no longer walk, you fly. You travel with the wings of freedom.

The truth is that in this world everyone is learning the lesson of forgiveness, through which everyone forgives themselves, God, everything, and everyone. The way this lesson is learned is, to some extent, irrelevant, because everyone is learning it, and they will learn it in one way or another.

Do not forget that the plane of space-time, the material realm, not only hosts the physical body, but also contains a reality beyond the body that remains part of the temporal universe.

III. You Have Chosen

The reality in which you experience life through your body is a perfect path to awakening. You wake up through the body. You know your true self through the body. The body is a means that serves the purpose of awakening. It is not the only means, but is the means chosen by God for you and for all who inhabit the physical dimension.

Is it not true that things like the body and the world are worthy of being loved, honored, and respected for what they are? The perfect means for your awakening to love in union with your mind, your heart, your soul, your being, and everything that inhabits the Earth and beyond?

We are talking about a divine relationship. Be aware that the spiritual paths that you have traveled to arrive here—from the path of the heart to that of knowledge—have ended. We start a new path now. To explore it together is what I prepare you for in this sixth book of the love letter that invites you to choose only love, to choose only your true being.

Being is pure discernment because it is pure consciousness. If you remain within the discernment of true reason—something you can do perfectly beginning here after completing the paths prior to this one—there is no danger of your getting lost in the world or in any other universe or dimension. Once you know who you are, and you accept that knowledge as the only truth about you, and you are determined to live in a conscious relationship with this that you now know, then wherever you go you will remain who you really are.

When I say that you have decided to live in relationship with what you have discovered as the only truth about you, I am saying that you choose to live within the divine relationship, within the reality of love. Accept that you are Christ. Accept nothing else. Accept that you are love and nothing but love, and that God, or the source of your being, if you prefer to call it that, is the one who instructs, guides, informs, drives, moves, and lives you. This is the same as saying that your will has joined that of your Creator by a deliberate act of your agency. This is how God becomes your joy and your fullness.

You are established by God and remain united with your Creator in a union that nothing can dissolve. Life cannot be separated from that to which it has given life. Thus you never stopped being the living Christ who lives in you even though you have traveled a path in which you thought you were something else.

Once you accept who you really are and live in harmony with it, what effect can death have on you? None. That is why the statement that death does not exist, nor does it have consequences, is perfectly true—there are no consequences for who you are. Ultimately in death nothing happens. What you are simply continues to be manifested and will continue to do so forever. Here you have the simplest and clearest definition of eternal life.

Just as recognizing your true Christ identity and living in union with it makes death cease to have meaning, the same happens with the illusion that the world has some effect on you. For those who have found the truth, creation is recognized as innocuous, and life as neutral. They know that the world of dualities, of cycles and changes, of beginnings and endings, has no effect on their being because they have no cause in God. They have not only discovered the treasure of their true being, but that discovery has led them to know that, being the living Christ, their being is the cause of everything, as they are being the effect of God upon it.

If Christ is the cause of who you are, in the sense that it is your origin and your being, then what is not similar to it has no cause. When this truth shines in your minds and vibrates in your hearts as those who have reached God on Earth, then you know that what is not love has no consequence. You have reached the holy indifference of the world.

Indifferent to all that is not love, the enlightened ones walk the Earth, sowing peace with their presence alone. They separate the tares from wheat with their holy discernment, so that the fields bear more and more abundant fruit and nothing obstructs the growth of what will become the bread of eternal life. They spread the seeds of the Kingdom where hearts are thirsty for beauty and truth. They give life at every step. They awaken souls. They live love in the manner of God. They do not confuse what love is with what it never can be. They do not disguise goodness for what is not, nor do they call things what they are not.

It is not for the holy to live with the profane. It is not for love to live in the house of fear. However, the holy can step on the profane Earth and sanctify it in the same way that love can enter where fear dwells and transform it into a dwelling worthy of Christ. Holiness and love can do that because they know what they are in union with their life-giving source. They know why nothing can change them. They know they can never cease to be what they really are. Not only do they know it, but they would never think of being anything other than what they forever are.

If what you are cannot change—and that only applies to who you really are—then where is there room for fear? Remember, all fear is the fear of not being. Hence the importance of understanding with perfect clarity what you are, not only with your mind but with your heart united in truth.

Once you love what you are, which is to say that you love Christ, then you stop fearing, for the simple reason that once you join the love that your being is and remain in it, you cease being afraid of losing love, the source of all fear. If you cannot lose yourself, then what real loss can you experience? What battle can reach the Kingdom where only the unshakable peace of the Creator of the holy, beautiful, and perfect reigns, and in which nothing else can exist? What fear can be justified once you live within the strength of God's spirit, where nothing untrue can reach?

You enlightened ones who love yourselves in the manner of God, and therefore who love everything that exists, do not fear the truth, whatever it may be, however it may manifest. This statement is essential to the path that you will travel from now on, increasingly in harmony with the will of the Father. The lie is the basis of the ego; the truth is the foundation of eternal life. That is why it is so important that you observe your mind and heart and make sure that you never discover in yourself anything that is untrue. Lying is not a characteristic of love. Telling the truth and nothing but the truth, at all times, places, and circumstances in which it is called to be told within the embrace of love, is living as those who no longer are identified with illusion.

Not infrequently the enlightened ones may seem heartless, although they are not. They live in the heart and their mind is linked to the truth, therefore they have abandoned madness if they were ever in it. They do not fall into the pattern of ego that presents itself as sensitive when it is but a game of emotions disconnected from truth. They do not cry for what makes no sense to cry about. They do not laugh at that which, by not proceeding from holiness, does not cause joy.

They are real. They do not act. They live thinking of God.

The way of being Christ now and always is the way of the truth in which you were created. Once you recognize this, not with the intellect but in spirit and truth, you cannot desire anything less than God. The high does not coexist with the low, just as the sky does not touch what is under the sea. The enlightened have learned to live with their feet on the ground and their eyes on the sky. They are not contaminated because they live in the eternal purity of their being. They speak only words of eternal life, of God's works, the fruits of holiness. They do not seek to please because they know that is impossible. They are the living expression of God.

Being the Christ you have always been is not something that changes because you are on Earth or in any other dimension of creation. Although you cannot stop being what God has arranged for you to be, what is sought here is for you to be aware of who you are. Being is not the same as accepting who you are and living in harmony with it. Being aware of the Christ being you are and allowing what you really are to express is all that should be called the art of living.

Does who God is cease to be because God manifests in time? Is God only true in the Kingdom of eternity? Can the truth cease to be what it is simply because it is part of matter and space?

Sisters and brothers of all time! The spatial-temporal dimension of creation is not an obstacle to the truth. Nothing is. Therefore, do not think that because in the past you did not find within yourself the love you were looking for, that love does not exist. Nor think that because you do not seem to dwell in endless bliss, that it does not dwell in you. Now you have awakened to love. You are no longer what you once were. I made something new of you. You need not complain about a past that is not here nor will ever be present again.

The time when you were governed by the forces of the body has been left behind. Now you rule everything that is part of you. You know that if you don't rule, then the body will. That is what happened in the past. But now you have claimed your power and your glory, and the movement of your spirit has given life to a new creation in you: a new being, a new reality, based on love.

Nothing can attack who you really are. Nothing can hurt who you are by divine disposition. Nothing can contaminate your holiness. Your innocence has been so sheltered from everything alien to it that nothing can taint it. You are the virgin, the saint, the redeemer, and the redeemed. You are the sweetness of love. You don't need others to tell you this. You know it. You need not prove it to anyone; know it and rest in that sacred knowledge every day of your life.

3.

Peace Has Come

*A message from Jesus speaking from both his Humanity
and Divinity, identifying himself as "the living Christ
who lives in you"*

I. My Love Belongs to You

Son of the wind! Daughter of the fire of love! What a joy it is to be certain! What a joy to live in the truth!

The firmament of your holy mind is now clear and you rest in the eternal peace of the Christ that you are. Peace has finally arrived.

Oh, eternal joy, unequaled joy, joy of redeemed souls! How sweet are the panoramas of the world when you look at them through the eyes of love. How beautifully we contemplate everything when seen with spirit and wrapped in the embrace of love.

Oh, holy God, eternal Father, how great are your works! You do everything right. You have given humankind the grace of divinity. You have made them return to love without prejudice to their freedom. You who are patient and loving without equal, accept this prayer that springs from our hearts united in spirit and truth, hearts in which all who long for peace reside.

Oh, saints unknown to the world, but known from all eternity to me and to my Father who is in Heaven! You have many reasons to celebrate. Wake up to the joy of God. Live consciously every day of your lives in the bliss of Heaven that you are. Every wisp of wind, every snowflake, every innocent look will tell you about me. I am tireless love.

Beloved humanity! I have been calling you for more than two thousand years. Before that I called you through the prophets. I have been calling since time began to roll, like a wheel that comes off its axle and keeps turning until it stops. I have looked for you in all the corners of the world. I have become your yearning for love so you do not forget me. I was present in the beauty of the birds of the sky and the lilies of the field. I have sighed for you in every moment of your life.

Immersed in an ecstasy of contemplation, in the embrace of my Sacred Heart, I cried when you turned your face and laughed with you when we gazed together at the sky. I raised you when you were down, and cradled you when your faith waned and your strength weakened. I held the lamp of my love every time you felt dejected and confusion took hold of you. I have loved you. I have instructed you. I created you. You are forever in my love. I am still loving you, instructing you, creating you.

I am your beloved Jesus of Nazareth, the son of sweet Mary. I am the one that many say they know, but they don't know me when they make me a marble idol, believing I am different from themselves in spirit and truth.

I am the one who, like you, was created a human to give a face to love; and having given it, I became one with God. I am the first among all humans of the world, the firstborn of God and your elder brother. I am the one who on countless occasions sent you my angels from Heaven to aid in your discernment and to keep you from falling off the precipice into the world's hallucinations.

I am the one who inspires you with the right word. I am the one who has sent you to all who have loved you, and they have done so in my name. I am that for which the soul sighs with holy love. I am the abode of light. In me, your being sings of joy and your heart dances with beautiful love. In my being, your mind rejoices in truth and all creation praises God, its Source and Creator.

Oh, light of Heaven! New life has arrived! Peace has come. Your arrival is announced with a heavenly hymn, a prelude to a love that will never cease. The angels of God sing it. It has arrived. The sovereign of Heaven is here, surrounded by seraphim and divine lights, whose beauty pleases the spirits that live in the harmony of holiness.

Oh, eternal sovereign, blessed peace, queen of everything created, source of love itself! You have reached the soul that is here, absorbing these words, which are a perfect expression of the wisdom of love.

Soul in love, together we have walked the paths of the world. Now we will walk the paths of Heaven. To you and to all who receive my voice expressed in this way, I say: Come, blessed of my Father, come to enjoy the delights of the peace of God that together we have achieved. Because you have reached the truth, nothing and no one will take away what is yours by birthright. I tell you: my love belongs to you.

II. The Sovereign of Being

Peace has come, love has overcome. The heart has reached what it longed for. There is nothing to look for anymore. Now we begin to express more vividly what we always were, although we did not always recognize it. Learning to do so is impossible because this is beyond all learning. But have no concern, since it is unnecessary to learn.

You were created with the ability to express God's peace in all its glory and beauty.

The truce has not only been signed, but peace is now your only reality. You who listen to my voice and follow it know you now live in peace, that the miracle of the resurrection has been performed in you. Remember that you are the one. Start with me now to enjoy who you are, to enjoy the feast of life. There is so much to be happy about! There is so much joy to share!

Oh, expression of love! How beautiful is your countenance. How sweet your voice. How smooth your walk. How graceful your look. How knowing your words. How bright your light. How beautiful your waist on which the seal of purity rests. How innocent your colors. How blessed your form. How holy your thoughts. How beautiful your feeling.

Beloved of my core, you have gained Heaven by abandoning yourself in me. You have entered the holy abode, in which your true mind resides, united with your heart. You are holy. You are the living expression of God on Earth and in Heaven.

The time has come for you to make the truth about yourself the only truth that interests you. Believe me when I tell you that who you are will accomplish great wonders in you and in the whole world. In effect, you are already doing them. Above all, remember that the works of the spirit are for Heaven and not for what is not eternal, even if they extend to it.

Your being resides in Heaven, because Heaven is you. Therefore, all you do when you remember the truth about who you are is to remember where sweetness dwells, where tenderness lives. Remember where you live.

Now that peace has come and you live in truth, observe the panoramas of Earth from the Heaven of your holy mind, and respond from the beauty and serenity of your heart until the day comes when you are no longer seen in a body, although you will be remembered forever by those who chose only love.

Now, looking from everything at a distance, and remaining immersed in the happiness which you long sought, is it not me that your heart was looking for? My love? Together we have lived for eternity, embraced in the unity of truth. Where life existed, in any of its forms, there we always were and will remain. We are the extension of holiness. We are the unity of being. We are creative light.

What is being said here, from the depths of heart, is that new times have begun for you and for humanity. The time of Christ's peace in you has begun, a peace unlike that of the world. It comes from Heaven and has been given to you. There is no need to fear conflict anymore because only truth is in you.

Your purpose—to find yourself—drove you to achieve this. You are powerful! So much so that you snatched Heaven for Earth. You have begun a new era in the consciousness of humanity, an era marked by a direct relationship with God, an era of the living Christs of God on Earth. It is the era in which humanity accesses a greater knowledge of God's love. It is the era of truth.

In our relationship lies all true meaning. Every relationship expresses something. If it is a relationship with truth, it will express truth, even if it is within illusion and manifests with the illusory. Truth is the source of all meaning. Thus to live so that life makes sense, where you have the certainty of your function in creation, you must live consciously in relationship with love.

A central aspect of how you live from now on, a new life in which peace is your only reality, is to understand that each one has a path to travel that it is perfect, since each is according to the design of the soul with the Creator. It matters not whether the paths of others make sense to you or not, whether they seem to have much suffering or none, whether they seem valuable or miserable. None of that matters. Put aside everything that is not Christ. Doing so is not abandoning your brother but abandoning yourself to love.

Those abandoned to the truth, which is the peace of God, think not about how to change their lives or the lives of others. Nor are they concerned about having those who are close them walk a certain path, for each soul has decreed out of time, in union with the will of God, to transit a particular mode of human life. Recognize that each soul belongs to its Creator. Do not seek entry where nobody and nothing can enter, for it is an inviolable space reserved only for the soul and God.

Peace and truth are one, and outside of truth there can be no certainty of any kind. That is why when you make the truth central, you can be reliable, even in the various environments of the world. You cannot trust the lie; nothing about it is certain. Hence fear arises. Now that you know that the lie can be unmasked, you need not feel insecure about anything.

Those who have found the truth, and that includes you, know that they can live serenely, as if walking through a dark forest with a bright torch lighting the way. The torch is the light of Christ, the light of wisdom restored to your holy mind. You need but shine it towards whatever you wish to see clearly, and appearances will be put aside and what was hidden will be sweetly revealed. You no longer need to teach anything, but if others ask, you will give from the sweetness of your heart and the generosity of your soul. When love asks, you will act as a patient parent who has let go of their attachment to learning; even if they need to keep repeating lessons for a child who needs more time to learn, they do it for love and with love. You live serenely because the sovereign of Heaven, the peace of Christ, now reigns forever in your heart, purified by the unction of the Father's love.

III. Peace is Now

As I have said, you are at the entrance to a new path that you will soon begin to consciously travel, the path of being. You can only travel this path after having finished the paths of the heart, of transformation, and of knowledge. This path, which is the destiny of the other paths, is the only eternal path because being who you really are is that for which you were created.

An essential aspect of this new path you are now entering, is that of no anticipation. Living in present love is God's way of life. God is not confused, thinking there is something forward called the future, when in reality it is imagined. Nor does God think about the past because that is not true mind. Remember, love does not think at all, it simply is what it is, now and forever. The same must happen with you from now on.

For love, once again I tell you: if the past weighs on you, do not think about it. I take care of the future. Live in the present in my love. This is the key to living in peace—living in such a way that the love you are is expressed here, now, and forever.

There is only one source of happiness: living the truth of who you are as God created you to be. So if you live in the present that love is, you will live without worries and dismantle forever the insane compulsion of the mind to anticipate things.

Speculative thinking is insane, as is everything that comes from the ego. In an attempt by the thinking mind to control things, it believes that if it anticipates, it will be able to change what is and what will be. That part of the mind is not real. It knows nothing about creating. The future is something we create together. In fact, it is something we are creating now. Simply put, in every moment you create time or stop creating it. You create illusion or stop creating it.

The thought pattern of anticipation is the source of psychological time-making from which the ego was historically nourished. It is the source of pain that occurs in besieged minds unable to rest in the serenity of now. That spiritual siege—the compulsion to make time by focusing the mind on thoughts of the past or the future—is something like a demon that suffocates the soul until you definitively tell it to leave and never come back.

Past memories do not interest those who will travel the path of being. Their only interest is in remembering God, that is, the love they really are. Why do they want only to remember what they are in the light of truth? Because they know that this is the will of their Creator. They live in relationship with their source. They make the sacred link with God the reason for their lives, the only object to which their minds and hearts are directed.

Anticipation is typical of the fearful. Anxiety, which is the result of spiritual siege, is nothing but fear coming from the whims of the ego. As we have said several times, the ego is gone. Peace has come. But now you have to learn to live in peace.

You have been told that you cannot teach the peace of God because it is teaching love, which is beyond all possible learning. Nevertheless you can learn to recognize, value, and embrace the conditions of peace.

Living in the present, immersed in the love of the living Christ who lives in you, is a condition for living in love, and therefore for peace. It is akin to the condition of breathing for the preservation of life. This truth is not a cause for worry, but something you should be aware of.

If you notice that your mind is lost in past ramblings or in speculations about the future, as soon as possible look for a calm place, breathe deeply, slowly, and consciously. Focusing your attention on the breath, say to yourself:

My love, essence of my being, a part of the mind has been lost. Let us gather it in. May everything return to the peace of Heaven. Let everything be embraced by the truth. May everything return to love. Amen.

When you have calmly observed that part of the mind which intermingled with the memory of the old madness in which it was hurt, and you have returned it to love, you will see how peaceful you are. Wrap everything in peace and there will be no signs of yesterday.

For one who lives in truth, there is no difference between that which occurred a second, a century, or a millennium ago. All past is simply that: past. The same goes for the future. It matters not whether the mind focuses its thoughts on what it will eat tomorrow, or what the body will wear upon waking, or if it will go to in a distant future.

You know all this yet I repeat it here at the gates of the new path because I do not want to take risks. Prudence is not a friend of the risk-takers but of those who live in the truth. Living in the present is the basis of traveling the eternal path of relationship with God.

That relationship is now, as is the peace of Heaven, life, and your being. At no other time than in the present can you be at peace. At no other time than now can you be aware of something, including this relationship. Whenever you disconnect from the present you disconnect from your Christ consciousness. Love and the peace of God cannot live in the future nor remain stuck in the past. Love can only be what it is now, being the eternal present. Be glad that this is so.

IV. Everything Is Perfect As It Is

Staying anchored in the present is essential for those who walk the Earth as the Christ of God. They understand that awareness of now, while still located in time, is so similar to eternity that both realities come together in an instant of love and truth. The present moment is such only when it is a "now" of pure love. That is possible to the extent that past, future, and all judgment are released. Present-love is when everything is allowed to be as it is in the certainty that everything is perfect as it is.

In order to live anchored in ever-present love, it is necessary to accept that the life of each one, as it is, is the perfect path that God prepared for each of Her children and for the collective as an expression of the covenant of the soul with its Supreme Creator.

Christ, the infinite relationship of all realities, holds within itself universal harmony. This means that the laws of love, which are what sustain life, are the basis upon which the universe works. That means everything. No part of creation is not linked with the rest. This relationship may not be seen, but that does not mean it does not exist. You can see its effects.

The union of the totality—divine union—and the present are the same on the plane of truth because truth is eternal, not subject to or conditioned by time. That is why the divine relationship is everything. In fact, God's relationship with everything created and everything created with God is the only real relationship. Other relationships, whether the relationship between the numbers of a mathematical equation, or between different ideas in a theory, or even between the value of relativity between two beings or their relationship with time, lack meaning when they are disconnected from divine union because they require union in totality.

Everything is linked to everything by love. The thinking mind can believe that it can create new mental interrelationships between things in a different way than God has established. This is what separation means: to establish a type of link that lacks a foundation in perfect love. The thinking mind is its own reality; with that it would create a world that by definition cannot join anything, as it conceives of it, so as not to lose itself in the totality, since it believes that being the same prevents the possibility of being different.

It is not for the mind to create reality. Life has been created by God and is eternal. When speaking of separation, or the loss of love, in reality what is being spoken of is living by a thought system whose foundation is the desire for autonomy, rather than lovingly accepting the fact that we are all interdependent, including the Creator. Can a Creator be such without a creation that She Herself created?

There can be no peace without truth. This is why, again and again, when we remember that peace has come, we speak of truth. In your mind, that part of your soul that lives together with the love of God, is the true reason of Christ. It is there where the beauty of reason dwells, where without exception all the treasures of the Kingdom are found. And there are so many! All of them are united like a beautiful bouquet of blessed flowers. Love, reason, truth, peace, harmony, creation—all are priceless pearls co-existing within your holy mind together with countless others.

Heart-centered living—in which reason and love remain united—is the way of Christ.

What I am saying is that the enlightened ones who have achieved the peace of Christ in this world are those who from their own very dissimilar experiences have internalized—made flesh—the fact that there is a Being superior to everything that exists; that this Higher Being governs creation; and that it is a Being of pure love from which everything arises eternally, including themselves. They know that this Supreme Being of pure love, which some call God, others Abba, Allah, Sun, Yahweh, or by countless other names, is the same holy love that surrounds all existence. This certainty which comes from the wisdom of the heart is the foundation of peace.

Everything that exists must have a basis upon which it rests. Just as a tree cannot exist without roots in the ground, or a house without a foundation, the same is true for all creation. Nothing exists by itself apart from the source of life that is God.

The sweet recognition that there must be a "something" that gives existence to everything, including you, is the basis for you always to live in the love of Christ. This recognition is not only a universal truth; it is also the basis upon which peace, joy, and beauty are built. It is the basis of life.

All life was created on the foundation of perfect certainty. Doubt is not part of divine reality. Does this not make sense? The significant point is for you to understand certainty.

The only certainty necessary is to recognize, with love and pure acceptance, that nothing and no one is autonomous, nor need be; that the relationship of everything with everything within the love of God is the reality of life. The only certainty necessary to recognize is that love is the only reality.

Accepting the divine relationship as the only reality within which everything exists is the precondition for peace because it is the condition for truth. Those who live remembering this truth every day until this memory becomes part of their way of being have abandoned loneliness and lack forever. If infinite love governs your existence, how can there be fear? Remember, where love is there is no room for fear. This remembrance of love is essential for those who incarnate Christ, for you who receive these words will very soon go out into the world in your holy ministry.

Love is the foundation of reason. Love is the abode of truth. Love, reason, and truth are a yoked unity that dwells in the heart of your soul, the center of your being. Love is not interested in living anywhere other than the sacred temple where truth dwells, because one is the essence of the other. Love cannot co-exist with illusion because love is pure reality and what is not real can never be accepted by reason as worthy of being venerated. Remember that veneration is a harmoniously embedded feeling in the love relationship that flows from the created to the Creator, and from no other relationship. Part of the holy panorama of divine truth is that the time in which humanity is living now, this new time in history, will be marked by the union of reason and love. That union that has not always been recognized or honored but it is the basis of soul life and creation.

To return to unity and to remain in divine relationship is to remain in the unity of reason and love. It is the state in which you live as the Christ you are, you feel what the Sacred Heart feels, and you think what the Divine Mind thinks. Once you recognize the sacred union that exists between love and reason, you begin to allow truth to be revealed to you. No effort or trial is necessary. You begin to allow the Christ you are to truly manifest itself because of the love it is. In that way you recognize that everything is perfect as it is, not according to the old thought patterns of ego, but according to the truth that comes from love and reason. This is how you joyfully recognize that peace has arrived. The sun shines again. The sky is clear. Christ has arrived.

4.

The Return to the Father

A message from the Voice of Christ through a choir of Angels, in the presence of Archangel Raphael and Archangel Gabriel

I. Daughters of Light

Beloved of Heaven! Mirror where holiness is reflected! We have come again before you, wrapped in light. We bring in our hands the Book of Life, a blessed gift from the One who has no name, the One who created all, the One with the arm of justice and love, the One who makes the light shine and the breezes blow.

We come full of joy and peace. We shine with the colors of the sky that give joy to the eyes of your soul. We are the angels of God who have come to dwell with humanity through you. We are sisters, brothers, friends, and also co-creators with you. We are messengers of love. Or rather, we are love expressing in a particular way, just as you do in your own way.

The angels of God come singing as choirs of Heaven. The redeemed souls arrive. They arrive before this blessed land, full of Heaven and love, the countless who have made the choice for love.

Hosana on high and joy on Earth! A new day dawns, a day when love shines as never before in your souls. Oh, perpetual novelty of love! Eternal creation of endless life!

Well-loved soul of God, sweetness of Christ, joy of the Mother of the living! Remember that you are already in Heaven by your decision of pure love made in the exercise of your free will. You have decided in union with the will of the Father to spread divine light in the world until the time comes for you to continue doing so without a physical body. At that moment you will continue to preserve your body in all its beauty but as a spiritual body, glorified and full of beauty, health, and eternity. It will be the perfect reflection of the light of your glory, beautified by the waters of eternal life.

Pure soul, in love with Christ, Daughter of the light! Start calling our sisters and brothers to come to the light. Christ is both coming and already here. Christ lives in each one of you holy souls that receive these miraculous words. We give you life in this work. We give you Heaven through the healing of memory.

Oh, saints of God who have remembered the love of love! You will not regret having given your time and your lives to truth. We assure you that you will receive one hundred for one. You will receive eternal life in return. You who have chosen only love will live forever in its presence because of your choice.

Living Christ, remember that every expression of love is necessary and sacred. Everything you do in your work for God is blessed by Heaven and bears abundant fruit. Nothing can be superfluous in your expression of your relationship with your source. Among those who have chosen only love, some sing, others write, pray, work, or dance. They all love in the way of Christ. They have made the decision to move with the love they feel for their Creator. The strength of their longing to do something for their Divine Beloved is so great that they have burst into an explosion of expression. More and more will you see on Earth their manifestations of beautiful love. Rejoice, for a new explosion of love has begun.

II. Back to Love

Daughter of love, you must know that, recognizing something with the thinking mind and accepting it as a truth that is part of your being are two different things. That is why we have traveled a path that touches both your heart and your mind. We, the angels of God, who by design of the Mother bring before you the voice of the living Christ, know that there is no such thing as a heart and a mind, for both are a single spiritual reality within the human soul. We use the words "mind" and "heart" because we integrate the language of separation, which is what emerges from the tower of Babel, and we transform it into a new language, the language of unity.

You are in a perfect position not to get lost in symbols, that is, to gather what the separation intended to separate and bring it to the center of the universe, the heart of God, or center of universal unity. That center, or place, exists.

When we speak of your divine reality, the truth that you are, we are referring to something that human language cannot describe but which, nevertheless, can be indicated by words. We have used words throughout history to describe the indescribable, to serve the purpose of truth. There is no need to obliterate human language to direct the mind and heart to Heaven. Pronounce the word "love" with all your soul, all your mind, and all your heart, then remain silent, and you will experience the mystery of life. Pronounce the word "God." Stay silent and see what happens in your heart.

Words are loaded with feelings, emotions, and beliefs, all of which have some effect on you. When evoking happens in you, it affects all of creation. That is why Jesus has told you that every word is significant. This is not a matter of concern, but a recognition of the power of the children of God. When we say that words affect creation we are referring to the thought that precedes them and its corresponding feeling. It is the union of thought and feeling that has power, not the word alone.

We have already recognized the power of the mind and also the power of feelings, and you know that in both lies an energy that creates your conscious experience. Therefore honoring your feelings and thoughts, as well as those of your sisters and brothers, becomes a fundamental basis for living as the Christ on Earth.

Love is inclusive. It integrates everything within itself and transforms it all into love. By embracing everything within love, everything is transmuted into a greater degree of loving consciousness. If you belittle your peers' feelings under the assumption that there are good or bad feelings, or sinful or holy thoughts, you engage in an activity so alien to creation that it disconnects you from the creative choir of God's children.

During the time when you governed your life through the thought system of separation, you used exclusion as a means of protection. You thought that when you separated yourself more, you were more different. By increasingly differentiating yourself, creating the unique individual you wanted to be, you considered your identity safe. Now you know this not to be true, and that the opposite is true. This recognition brings you back to the truth of who you are. It returns you to the Father's house.

Returning to the Father's house is an expression that refers to the return to the Divine Love that your being is, to your true identity as a well-loved child of God. It is in the parent's house that you learn who you are, are given an identity, given a name, and where you absorb the thoughts, beliefs, and values that make up your vision of life. If this is so in the family house on Earth, it is because in it is a remembrance of celestial truth. "Father's house" is an expression that symbolizes the origin of life and of your being.

Since what gave you life is what defines who you are and extends its nature to you, you are related to your source. That relationship of being with source is a divine relationship. It is what you are.

You are not only one with your source but also with the relationship between it and what you are. Recognizing this frees you from the fear of loss, loneliness, and abandonment. It allows you to return to love and remain within it.

In the parable of the prodigal son, many focused on the house but not on the father himself. Now that you have traveled the paths of the heart, of transformation, and of knowledge, you can focus your gaze on the essential. To do so literally recovers spiritual vision.

See how we are increasingly moving from form to content, from what is outside to what is within ourselves, from the surface to the depth.

A house is not the important thing. It does not affect who you are. What gave you your Earthly identity, regardless of whether or not it was self-centered, has been the relationship you have had with those who have served in some way as your "parents" regardless of whether they were really your parents or a single parent or even an institution.

In this context the word "father" refers to that from which you nourish yourself and obtain an identity, a way of being. Observe that in the human "family," regardless of the form it takes, there may be many children and each has a unique personality trait even though all have the same parents or educators.

What your identity gives you, regardless of whether real or illusory, is your relationship with life. It is not life, nor parents, nor culture, nor education, nor the world that defines who you are and therefore your responses. It is the relationship you have with everything that determines your responses, not the other way around.

III. Your Relationship with Life

Relationship causes your experience, not vice versa. When you experience something, you must first have established a relationship in your mind which defines a meaning, and based on that assigned purpose, creates an effect on your heart. The effect was the one sought for, so the relationship was assigned a purpose.

For the mind to assign a meaning to a relationship according to what it determines to be valuable leaves the relationship without purpose. All isolation arises from a belief that the relationship is without value. From this belief emerged the idea of separation from God. Believing that the relationship with what life gave you is of no or of little importance cuts off any link with life. The source of your life not only created you but sustains you and creates you eternally. You are not just the eternally created one, but are eternally being re-created. This distinction is of the utmost importance to you as you go through the world in an increasingly visible and eloquent way as the incarnate Christ.

You are not created, you are creation. Focus on this statement. Stay in it in the silence of peace that has no opposite. Immerse yourself in the deep chasms that this truth contains. Well understood, all truth lies in it. From it emanates humility. When you accept that you are creation, you recognize that

God's way is to constantly create your being. You do not exist at any other time than in the present, in God, because there is nothing else.

Love is eternally present, as are you. Thus you are love in such a way that the person you have been, even what you were a few minutes ago when you started reading this session, literally has ceased to exist. You are a new being in every moment. God is eternal creation, always creative and creating. Life does not age. Life is eternally nascent. To some extent we can say that you die every moment and are reborn every moment in a death that is not death but eternal life, and in a rebirth that is pure infinite joy.

If relationship is everything and there is no relationship outside the relationship with love, since love is everything, then we can say that this work leads you to the only truth to which you need to return, the direct relationship with love. This helps you to understand the sacred nature of this time of the new humanity of which you are a part, a humanity whose awareness of the direct relationship with God is foundational.

Spirits are opening to the direct relationship with love that their Creator is in a way that never happened before except at the origin of time. This opening to the love that resides in each heart, by the mere fact of existing, is the return to the Father's house. The house is the heart that God gave you; the Father is the love that God gave you; the son is the being that God gave you. Can you see how much your Father who loves you so much has given you? Can you start growing more greatly in love with who you are?

I hope with all my heart that by now you have noticed that the voice that speaks to you in these words is your own divine voice. It is the voice of your true consciousness. It is your being speaking to you and the whole world. It is the voice that you have been given as an extension of the living word so that the world hears a different way to love itself.

Ultimately this is the purpose of your life: to express a relationship with God in your own way based on your unique way of being. If you do not do so, you are not really expressing yourself. If what you express is what others believe or what others have experienced as if that were the only form of expression and that you cannot have your own experience of God, then you are denying your relationship with God and thereby denying your being.

The denial of your being is really the negation of a direct relationship with your source. In the autonomy or separation thought system, a being without a cause has to be God or nothing. You know that only God is the main cause of everything, including Himself. If it doesn't have another cause, then it would be God. In other words, if you are your origin and your cause, then you are like God, according to the thought system of separation. That is why separation was conceived, to be like God.

Does this sound a little familiar? Recall the Biblical dialogue with the serpent, who wanted to hide the truth by saying "you will be like Gods."

Those who seek to be like God are left without cause and therefore without a source of life, because in order to be like something you must be an imitator and not an authentic being. To be like someone is to imitate them since they are living from a comparison. If you imitate anyone, you don't have a cause. Imitation has no intrinsic roots. It has simply an external source which it seeks to copy.

Imitation is something like a drifting identity—not really an identity, but simply a copy of something. Imitating God has been the ego's game. Being authentically as you were created is the gift of love.

To believe that you cannot have a personal relationship with God, with angels, and with realms beyond the body and mind is to deny an existing and direct relationship. That belief is part of the past and now unnecessary. It is impossible for some to have greater access to divinity than others. Some express the relationship in one way, others in a different way. Well understood, life itself is an expression of a relationship with the Creator.

The question then, is how is your relationship with love now? Is it a distant relationship? Is it a scary relationship? Does it encompass your whole reality? Do you constantly turn to it to nourish yourself with divine nectar that gives life to your soul? Do you feel the love that lives in you? Do you feel at peace with yourself? Do you resort to peace as an inseparable friend with whom you share your dreams, your desires, and your life? Do you trust love? All these questions are one and the same: What does love mean to you?

Do not believe you cannot know the meaning of love. You can, because God is love and knowing Her is also knowing Her purpose as Creator of everything. Certainly this is not something that the thinking mind can comprehend, given its limitations. But you are not that, nor the thoughts you think you think, nor the desires you think you want. You are more than all of that. You are not a body struggling to survive, or having the best time possible before your inexorable death. You are spirit.

For you who receive these words the struggle between body and spirit has long since ended, which is why peace now reigns in your heart and will forever. Nothing and nobody can take your peace away. Actually, there was never anyone who could, not even yourself. It was really your own decision to disconnect from peace, but that didn't make the sovereign of your soul cease to live in your heart. It was not from peace, nor from love, that you separated, but from your own being. And since the treasures of the Kingdom reside there, when you disregarded the "nonsense" of your heart you disregarded everything that inhabits it.

How can you enjoy the peace of Christ if you turn your back on your heart?

The affairs of the heart are the affairs of your Father who is in Heaven. As we have said in this work, those are the issues that you have to deal with. Taking care of your heart is your only responsibility because your heart is what you are. By taking care of your heart you take care of your being. To take care of your being is to love yourself. Nobody takes care of what they do not consider valuable. Here you can find the staff of discernment that will keep you anchored to unchanging truth: How is your heart? What is happening in it? How well do you keep your blessed heart safe and sound? What dwells in it, fear or love?

IV. The Light Has Come

Knowing the meaning of love is perfectly possible by knowing its effects. You will recognize everything by its fruit. Confusion about the meaning of love lies in the fact that many wish to put it into words or give it a particular form when in reality it cannot be limited to form. Form is effect, not cause. While it is true that cause and effect are the same, it is also true that they are different. Being the same in being and different in relationship is the only authentic means of identification that God has created.

Focusing on form rather than on content is the basis of the old fear-based system of thought. Now that you live in love, you can avoid all confusion. When you recognize that perfect love dwells in your heart and you remain united to it, taking care of the affairs of the heart, the way in which love manifests itself will be somehow irrelevant. Even though you will express it without doubt because your only presence in the world will be a living extension of your being, you will not be focused on it. You will be focused on unity.

Being focused on unity rather than on form means that you will discover that your only function is to keep your heart within the light of your consciousness. To be fully aware of your heart is to achieve enlightenment. This means that you must be attentive, that is, observing without judging every thought, feeling, emotion, impulse, desire, reaction, response, or anything that arises in you. Such observation intertwines your being with your consciousness. This links you together with Christ and therefore with love, with the source of life.

You will meet new sisters and brothers each day on the new path that you will soon begin to walk. They are those who, out of time, made a pact with you and with God to meet in time to reinforce the presence of Christ on Earth. You will observe that your life will begin to feel as if you had hatched, like an explosion of life in which your expression begins to be discovered. After so many years of instruction, of preparing the mold and the dough, the yeasted bread bakes and will now begin to rise. The time of discovery of you by others has begun. This work will be the mainstay through which this takes place.

The expression of our divine relationship, which encompasses much more than these words, will arouse interest throughout the world. All those who since eternity have been created as the holy constellation of Christ's love will gather to illuminate Earth and Heaven. Those who meet through this work and every work that springs from our union meet with me because we are one mind, one holy heart, one being. Remember that these words are spoken from heart to heart, from being to being. They arise in the Heaven of your holy mind, where all who have made the choice for love reside.

Although not a single mind nor a single heart will fail to be reached by this manifestation of eternal life, some will resonate with one type of manifestation, and others with another. Love has infinite forms of expression and all of them are necessary, inviting others to love and express their authenticity. Thus, this work will touch hearts that since eternity have been looking for a type of spiritual energy or vibration to join. That force or frequency is what these words create. Other manifestations will create other frequencies, all emanating from the source of beautiful love, therefore identical in origin yet different in expression.

Each time a heart and mind join the vibrational frequency that these words create, they will be carried by the waves generated by this movement of love. Each will be moved and come to the light, to the surface to be seen by others. You might imagine this work as a powerful trumpet that angels sound with a call for the children of light to come to light, a call that resonates throughout the world. This is not a mere metaphor. It is true.

You who have read these words since the beginning of this work know that what is said is true. You know that you are not the same as you were at the beginning. You have changed. My love has transformed you. You have been carried by the wind of my spirit. These words have touched your heart, bringing a memory of a love without beginning or end. They fill your soul. Your heart sings and dances to the beat of my voice because you recognize who is speaking.

You have chosen the best part that will not be taken from you. You who have chosen only love are an essential part of this work. Without you these words would not exist, nor would Heaven exist. You are a receiver of Heaven.

Remember that what God gives is to be shared. Therefore you will also share what you have received for the goodness of Heaven through this angelic expression because your heart will sing happily whenever you share the wisdom of love with your sisters and brothers. As a pure soul united to eternal love with whom God Herself has made a covenant of love for which you have joined Her, you have the right to be happy. To do this you must claim your birthright to live in the joy of sharing. Sharing what you have discovered here will be your joy for all eternity.

I assure you that when you decide to share what you are in relation to God, you will say just as your Divine Mother out of pure love one day said to you: "All generations will call me happy, because the Almighty has done great wonders in me." From you will sprout a bliss that you have not known before on Earth, a peace long forgotten, a love that seemed lost but now is found.

If you knew how eagerly creation awaits your particular expression of God's love, you would hurry to recognize the living miracle you are and the holiness that lives in you. Angels await expectantly. Already they flutter in the sky and surround you everywhere, beating their wings with joy, flying the majestic flight of Christ. They come from all dimensions, gathering around you to see the work of God. They come from all the angelic universes to contemplate the wonders of the children of God. They come to praise the Creator for having blessed them with the grace of your expression of being.

Oh, child of Heaven! Holy creation! If you knew the beauty you are and how much joy your soul experiences sharing it, you would live happily forever. There is no beauty greater than the holiness given you by pure Divine Love upon your creation. Nothing and no one can ever defile it.

Oh, divine light of your holy being! My children! You who have chosen me, because I chose you first! Let your light illuminate everything. Begin to shine so that the world becomes more and more luminous. Remember that light does not come from the world but from Heaven. Allow the sun of your pure souls to illuminate everything, as you create Heaven on Earth. Within the light of holiness you create a new world based on love.

The time has come. Before you realize it, you will begin to shine as never before. It is God's promise!

5.

Talking to Heaven

A message from Jesus, identifying himself as "the living Christ who lives in you"

I. Heavenly Voices

Blessed soul of pure light, divine creation! Glorious child of the wind, what joy to have you with me forever. Contemplating you is my joy. My love for you never sleeps.

Oh, divine relationship! Cause of all love, bliss, and beauty! Holding hands we will walk the path of eternal life.

We are the light that illuminates nations. United we are the fullness of being. Rays of purity that embrace everything that exists arise from our union. The birds sing in honor of your return. The flowers give away their colors to brighten life. A small drop of water splashes in the pond. Stillness embraces everything. Silence becomes the sovereign of creation. Contemplation, the reason for existence.

Oh, Divine Love! Gift from , holy grace, treasure without equal!

Soul in love, voice that spreads the word of eternal life! Sweetness of love!

What bliss to realize that you have started a direct conversation with the heights! Communication with Heaven is present in these words that express the reality of your relationship with Christ, which is love.

Love calls you. Love speaks to you. Christ is your being, expressing.

Every time you join with what these letters, words, phrases, and sentences symbolize, you bring to your consciousness the reality of the love that you are. You become more aware of your relationship with the source of your being. As you have been reading you have felt many things, and a whole world has moved within your holy soul. Your heart trembled in the serene depths of peace upon hearing the sweet voice of your Divine Beloved. The mind rejoiced in the memory of your first love, and your soul began to fly back home.

You have been transformed by love. You have been reborn from above. The past is past. You are a new being, a truth you recognize not only with your mind but also with your heart. Now you feel the tenderness of your being. You know where the light dwells, where beauty dwells, where to find the wisdom that so pleases a mind and soul that loves truth. Now you know who you are.

Knowing what you are and being what you are, are really the same. For the moment, the knowledge of who you are seems to enter through your mind. Thus you point your finger to your blessed head, and look up to see beyond the body, a little above in the space around you, from which the flow of knowledge comes, pure joy that comes not from the world. And yet the mind and the heart are a unit. Therefore it matters not if truth seems to enter through a thought reflected in the mind, or by a feeling manifested in the heart. Remember, we call mind that from which all thought arises, and heart that soul space from which feeling emanates.

Because the mind and the heart are a unit, and I assure you that they are, it makes no sense to continue distinguishing between thinking and feeling. Both are the same, although their expression is experienced differently. But they are not different;

both come from the same center of your being. To say that you will only be guided by your feelings, leaving aside reason that has feelings join with wisdom, would be as harmful now as it was before, disconnecting intelligence from love. Remember, now that you have returned, nothing can be left out of the consciousness of love.

When you live in the Father's house because you have chosen only love, there is no reason to continue living as if you were a homeless orphan. The time has come to recognize and accept the truth unconditionally. You are everything that is part of your being: mind, heart, soul, spirit, and expression. You are also will, understanding, and creation. All that constitutes yourself. They are not separate parts, even though known in various ways. You are a whole. What you are is as sunbeams are to the sun; the expression of who you are is a ray of light emanating from the perpetual sun of your being.

II. Causality

This work is a call. It is an adamant invitation to stop seeing yourself as you will be, and to start living as what you are eternally. It is true that one day I said that I am who I am, and you are who you will be. That was said because it was like that at the time. But you were also told that there is a time for everything. Transformation is for time, not for truth.

There is a reason why you found these words. You have come here by the unfathomable design of the mind and heart of God, in union with you. You called me and I answered. I have looked for you and you let yourself be found. You gave me your soul, and I gave you my being. Nothing happens by chance.

The resistance, acceptance, and any other feelings or thoughts you have had throughout the reception of these words are part of knowing yourself in relation to God. Ultimately this is why this living expression of Divine Love exists: to act as a catalyst, moving the depths of your being like a wind that blows upon the ocean, creating water currents that allow it to remain pure, or like the moon, always beautiful and pure, that exerts on the serene waters of the sea a force that makes them dance, creating waves that come and go, thus giving life to everything that lives.

What would waters be without movement? The whole sea is in motion. Nothing within it is entirely still; not a single cell or atom lives without constant motion. Movement is the dance of life and has an echo in the soul.

These words create movement in your heart and mind. They come from the source of life, the source of movement. Within your being, the waters of your crystalline consciousness have moved. You are no longer the same. You have completed a path. You have reached a very specific place. You have come to the full recognition of your direct relationship with God, and you begin to manifest that relationship to create in union with love.

Every true relationship implies union or it is not a relationship. But coming into contact with someone or something does not mean you join it. The same goes for your being. Along this path we have traveled together, you have gone from understanding what you are to being what you are; from talking about love to being the love that talks. If you are in contact with God, however, you must be in union with Her: you have become one with who you are. This union will allow you to speak more clearly about yourself.

Now I ask you with all the love of my heart that you definitely give up what you once thought you were, thought you should be, or wanted to be. I ask you to accept that you and I are one, that there is nothing in your beloved Christ, in your beloved Jesus, in your beloved, always pure Mother Mary, that does not reside in you. I ask you to allow what you have received to nourish your mind, your heart, your memory, and your will so that the seeds of truth that we have sown together in the Eden of your soul continue to bear more and more fruit to be seen by those who are tired of the desolate but illusory views of the world, and therefore do not find peace even though peace has arrived.

You have traveled a path of knowledge and have reached perfect knowledge. I call you now to live in harmony with what you know you are. I invite you so that you may live in the fullness of being, and therefore in the happiness that cannot be taken from you. Your joy, your peace, your gaze, and your voice will reflect the holiness you are and the divine being in which the body dwells. Thus you will awaken others to love and you will experience having been created by love to live in the joy of giving.

Those whose hearts yearn for peace, those who fight for a better world, even those who condemn God for having created a painful, meaningless world will join you, and join in love. They will do so because they are of the truth and truth is limitless. Every time you decide to live in the reality of love, you activate the memory of truth in other minds and the remembrance of the first love in other hearts.

What you are now is a perfect, necessary, and essential expression of the love of Christ. You may have had other expectations for your life. Or you may find that, upon attaining enlightenment, you would do other things or experience extraordinary things worthy of being told for generations to come. If that is the case, I ask you to give up all such ideas.

Love knows nothing of form, even though it can be embedded in them. The secret of the relationship with God lies not in mystical visions or hearing voices that others do not, or knowing what others do not. The secret of divine relationship lies in the love that it is and in nothing else. Is it not worth growing more and more in love, allowing love to widen your heart so that you rise in holiness, instead of continuing to believe in a love so chimerical and small that it is not worth living?

Love is not what you thought it was. You already know this; you have experienced it. Therefore now is the time to live in union with that knowledge and allow it to manifest itself because of what it is. You are not a being who will soon cease to exist. You are not a gear within a machine destined to undergo what others have. You are a child of God, subject to love.

Begin to accept that love is a vivid force that cannot be neglected or set aside. You cannot make love insignificant, for it is the force that governs life. You know this because together we have been sharing in a clear and conscious way through this celestial work, as we bring love to the world. These dialogues are like a sweet conversation we share on a sacred mountain, a loving exchange between dear friends that flows from heart to heart, from one soul in love to another soul in love. This dialogue need not cease because we will soon begin a new path; it will continue forever.

I will never stop making my voice heard in hearts thirsty for love and truth. My voice is food for the soul, my wisdom is blessed nourishment for the holy mind. Truly, truly I tell you, if my word stopped manifesting you would cease to exist, no book of life would record your existence in the universe, no mind could remind you. My voice is the breath of spirit, the vital breath that gives life to everything that exists, the source from which all light emanates. It is what makes your soul cry, laugh, sing, dance, and wait for your beloved.

My word is life. It makes pure hearts sing. It gives peace to minds that seek rest. How could I stop giving life to my children through my word if they would faint without it? Beloved child, can you begin to realize the value of these dialogues? Of the eternal treasure that is the time we spend together, you and I, united in love through these words of eternal love, of endless life?

III. Universal Relationship

The tone of these dialogues is different from other writings not only because you are a unique being, but because humanity as a whole is no longer what it once was. Within the consciousness of the new humanity are new forms of expression. Remember, all that exists is consciousness; nothing exists outside it.

I invite you now to take a little tour with me of the history of humanity, because in it you will remember your own history and that of creation. We proceed in a simple way, without stridencies or complex concepts that may cause confusion. We will do this from the perspective of love, love that lives eternally together with reason.

Although it is true that you are not your story, it is also true that your heart has an inherent tendency to seek its origin, for as has been said, the soul always returns to its first love which is God. In observing the history of creation including humanity from this perspective you will begin to take some distance from the past, so that the road we will begin to travel will be cleared of predetermined ideas.

Humanity, and with it the soul, came to the world of time from a dimension outside of time. Time is not eternal, unlike the Kingdom of Heaven, which is. After being was created in the eternity of the Father of Lights, the soul went into a state of condensed, limited consciousness, a contraction in which it "experienced" the state of amnesia of which we have spoken.

Naturally, for this experience to happen, an entire universe had to be created. Remember that consciousness experiences itself to know itself. In effect, experience is "collected and created" by consciousness.

In the realm of the non-eternal universe there are three dimensions.

The realm of separation—if you prefer to use that expression, or of differentiation through disunity—is a temporal realm, but not everything in it is physical and spatial. From a state of deep amnesia the soul passes into a state of remembrance of itself. In the initial plane, there is time but not space; there is no matter. Some have tried to explain this dimension from whence the soul comes to the space-time universe as "past lives," or the concept of reincarnation. Thus the belief in karma was born.

The second state can be observed in the plane of time and space. Coming from the temporary state without space or matter to the physical plane as you know it now, you have actually elevated your being, in the sense that you passed to a greater degree of knowledge of who you are and of what creation is. We could say that you went from almost complete isolation to a greater degree of awareness of relationship.

To move from an isolated state of consciousness to the state of knowledge of the existence of relationship, you walked a path. First you related to your body, which if properly understood is a relationship with something beyond you, and therefore is a start towards a relationship with the whole. After a while you began to relate to the environment that surrounds the body. Along that path within the realm of time and space you move into a consciousness in which you transcend the body while remaining in the spatial universe.

On the space-time plane or path of the bodily world, you grow in the awareness of relationship. First you relate to what you somehow perceive as what life gave you. Usually you call it "mother." Then you expand and relate to "another me," often called "father." Then you relate to "other selves," usually the family. Later you broaden the spectrum of relationships and develop links with many more selves, the society in which you live.

Can you start to see how the way of humanity—and that concerns the collective as well as the individuals, since they are a unit—is but a journey towards a greater knowledge of the breadth of relationship? A walk from a coarseness of being towards a growth in consciousness?

The first humans—your brothers and sisters far away in time but united in holiness with who you are because they are an essential part of the mind of Christ and the heart of God— certainly had a degree of relationship much more limited than yours today. No matter how much effort they made, they could not know the wide panorama of Earth, much less the vision that you have from the clouds above what you call your home.

The impulse of humanity to occupy all the spaces of the Earth, and even to explore other worlds, comes from the inherent need of the soul to reach the divine relationship, a relationship with the whole. Truly, truly I tell you that the heart of humanity will not rest in peace until the happy recognition of the divine relationship is reached. And you cannot do so without first walking a path of purification of both the bodily and spiritual senses, both of which are mental.

It is always necessary on this path of purification to get rid of the false associations that the mind and heart have woven around the meaning of relationship. Enlightenment is a state that is reached after a purge of false beliefs. It is actually a process whereby an understanding of the nature of essential relationship is achieved. Let me say it sweetly but clearly: when you realize that relationship is sacred and you accept relationship as the fundamental stone upon which truth exists, you are enlightened. Never before. Two thousand years ago I expressed this by showing what others later called the mystery of the Holy Trinity, even though what was meant was simply that God is relationship, is love.

The fact that a truth as simple as this has been the subject of so many discussions over the centuries, with humans seeking to understand with the thinking mind the meaning of the Holy Trinity, demonstrates how difficult it is for the ego to understand relationship.

If relationships in the world are difficult for the thinking mind to understand, even more so will be the divine relationship, which is nothing other than the relationship with all that is true—the relationship with the All of everything.

Relationship is the means and end of knowledge. For this were relationships created. That is why one day I told you that relationship was created for you to be happy. Since you cannot be happy without knowing yourself—for the simple fact that happiness is what you are—then it is obvious that relationship is what allows you access to the bliss for which your heart longs.

At this point on the path you can clearly understand that relationship is the center of the life of being because consciousness realizes its reality in relationship with everything that is. Isolation hurts; it amounts to an annulment of being. Egocentric relationships generate pain because they are limited relationships, not sufficient for the being to fully know itself. In fact, ego-based relationships are relationships with illusion or fantasy since they are but related to an idea—never to the truth—of another being.

Seen from the perspective of relationship, you can understand the movements of humanity and God. I speak now of a relationship that has nothing to do with the relationship between bodies, but about your relationship with God—your being with the truth.

While being a social being in the world is an important achievement on the path to broadening the consciousness of universal relationship, the truth is that it is still a limited relationship. It is as if you decide to relate to a ton of grains of sand, instead of relating to every grain on the planet.

Not only with the intellect but with the heart do you grow with these words in the experience of your relationship with Heaven. By this I mean that you begin to realize in a very concrete way the Heavenly voice that is speaking. You recognize the voice. You remember it. Something inside tells you that you know it. A movement in your heart wishes to continue listening to the voice that speaks to you of love and reveals the beauty of who you are.

You can only know your being in relation to truth because your being is true. You can only know yourself in truth within your relationship with me because I am truth. This is why you feel peace and the embrace of love when we spend this time of pure discernment together. We are both united in the pure abstraction of love. We are a divine relationship within the unity of being of everything created. Sisters and brothers from all over the world, what I am saying here is that the return to love is the return to your relationship with the divinity that you are. That relationship sets you free because in it you are the truth.

6.

The Creator Created

A message from Jesus, identifying himself as "the living Christ who lives in you"

I. I Am Creation

You have come to the world to remember relationship. This is why this world is so marked by relationship. Indeed, both humanity's central problem and its salvation lies in relationship. Wherein the error occurs is also the solution.

If you fully understood that your relationships must be enlightened relationships—that is, relationships between gods of pure love, between beloved Christs who love with one love which comes from the Christ of all Christs—you would thank God for having created you in relationship. To raise the understanding of relationship to the level of divinity is to elevate your being to the abode of Christ. The divinity that you are cannot relate other than in the manner of God.

Let us replace the word "God" with "love." Your loving being cannot relate but by love, with love, to love. In other words, the divine relationship is but the love relationship you have with yourself to the totality that you are. From that relationship of perfect love with who you really are extends your creations of love through the creative power of your being—just as creation extends from the perfect love relationship that the Mother has with Herself.

Love yourself in the manner of God and you will create universes of love and truth whose beauty is so incredible that you will be unable to find any other source of joy than creating more love.

The finger of God is touching the central point in this matter of the soul. In it lies all perfect knowledge.

Listen to me attentively and with love. The infinite bliss to which your being is called can only come from creating; for that it was created. Love is endless creative power. To understand this is to understand the essence of truth, for it is to understand the life of the soul and the reason for its existence.

If you are one with God, you are one because of one reality, one truth. You exist because of the creative power of the Creator. When I say that God is love and nothing but love, I am also saying that He is creation, and nothing but creation.

The joy of God lies in creating love eternally. So too for your being. To return to love or to choose only love is to return to the source of creative power that resides in you and to remain in it. Love is such a great power that to join it alone creates unimaginable effects. Yet the mind is accustomed to assigning itself minimal functions and thus ended up believing it was little, almost nothing.

When you know that for which you were created and where your source of bliss resides, you will experience a new difficulty. But do not worry, it will be for a very short time. When you observe the pain of not being able to understand what your function of creating new love means, you will realize that it comes from a fear, and let it go.

The fear of not understanding is a basic fear for the egoic mind. Since you already know what to do with these fear patterns of the old way of thinking which is alien to the truth of your Christ mind, you can simply let it go, saying:

"I have seen the thought pattern and I free myself. That is not what I am. It is simply a character. I forgive it, I let it go freely. I wish it peace. I am free. I am love. I am creation."

You will see how once you do that, peace begins to return to your mind and heart. From that peace is where you create the new love. Here is the answer to the question of how to carry out your mission within creation.

For you who receive these words and have chosen only love, God must be the eternal creation of pure love, and nothing else. What does this mean? It means that from now on you will release your ideas about God, to be replaced by this truth.

You have heard many things about God. Now you are asked to leave all that behind. I even ask you to be willing to abandon the idea of the Father God, of the triune God, of the God of love which I myself presented and demonstrated. Now I ask you to begin to allow the wisdom of Heaven to mold your Christ self so that the Christ of God completely takes on the human form that you are.

As a human being of nature—a gift from God—you are an eternal creator of new love. Indeed, if you cannot be that, then it would be impossible to be one with God. God is Creator. And this makes all the difference: to say that God is the creative power and Her child is the act of creation, that power and action are a unity, is to say truthfully that they exist in relationship.

II. God's Idea

You are no longer a child. You are a soul that has returned to the holy abode. You have returned to the truth that love is. Is it necessary to continue believing in a God, however wonderful that belief may seem, who does not satisfy the deep longing of your being? God is nothing that you thought. God is creative power, eternally creating new love.

You have been told that you can only create in union with me because you can only create in peace, since peace is where truth and love, the foundations of all perfect creation, reside. If creation were not based on truth and love, it could not be sustained in existence.

In order to continue creating new love in every moment as a perfect extension of the flow of eternal life to that which channels that power and shapes its expression, you must make peace the reason for your existence. Those who are at peace create new love.

This revelation reveals that love itself is always new. This has been said before, but now I relate it directly to the reality of what God is. If you still believe that God is a person outside of you, seated on a majestic throne somewhere in the universe, contemplating His creation to see how to resolve the cosmic mess that went wrong, you cannot be aware of the wonderful capabilities of your being which surpass any talents you could imagine.

The reason why a vision of God like the one described above will not help is because, although you think that "Lord God" is very loving, and that He loves you, which is already great progress, you will continue to see God as alien to you. You will not identify with Him. Such a vision of your creative source is as if you will now begin to see animals, plants, stars, and the wind, as something loving, whereas before you saw them as fearful. That first step makes you quite calm and able to walk decisively towards truth, because it comes from forgiveness. You know you are not a tree, the wind or the sea. The wind is the wind, you are you, and I am who I am.

We are all creative acts of creative power. We are love expressed. Being one with God means that the generative source of life gives existence to and sustains your being. When the new being you are jubilantly discovers this understanding of God, then you can understand where you come from, your power, your role, and the joy of your soul.

If you read these words carefully, especially those manifested in this session, you will also understand the source of any existential conflict. You will understand the path of humanity and your path in this blessed universe, so full of beauty and light.

Ultimately, returning to source means recognizing that the source resides in your being and is what gives life, and that both are a whole. If that is true, and I assure you it is, then what need have you to deal with an alien God who, no matter how loving He may be, cannot be one with you? That which is alien to you cannot be linked to your being, just as two bodies cannot unite even given the love they profess.

God and I are one. That is the affirmation that you must give to your mind and heart constantly until this truth becomes one with you, so you can truly say that truth and I are one.

You and your source are united, and this source of divine creative power is so similar to God that there is no distance between the Creator and your source. Yet the thinking mind seeks to shape the truth. The mind will try to understand this with its usual system of "if this, then that" conditional thinking. But no answer is satisfactory because your creative power is unlimited. You are one with your source, and your power is the perfect extension of the Creator.

Unable to understand, the thinking mind will seek to create situations that make this truth not understandable as manifest in form. Although this divine truth, once accepted, extends to the plane of form and will create a new world, it will not be realized in how the old way of thought, dominated by the egoic mind, could imagine. It will be accomplished according to the living Christ who lives in you.

The best way to avoid falling into the typical patterns of the conditional mind is to be aware of content rather than form. Let the truth being revealed to you do for you what you have been called to do for all eternity. The truth knows the truth. Put no limits on the power of your being. Do not define what we are discovering, but stay in a loving attitude of expectation. In other words, quietly watch and wait.

Another reason the thinking mind raises concerns about this discovery of your creative power and resists changing its ideas of God is because of its belief that it must participate in the creation of whatever the truth is. Just as the intellect did not have any volitional participation in the creation of your being, that is, you arose from God and not as a result of a mental exercise, likewise your being does not need the thinking mind to create. This scares the intellect, always so eager to meddle in the life of God. It tries to make a powerful contribution to the truth but it never can, because truth does not need assistance. What can contribute to everything?

We will not conclude this sixth book of this work of Heaven without springing the hinges that hold the mind to an idea of God that must be set aside. We will move towards the fullness of the unlimited truth that you are.

III. Reality and Meaning

Everything created, including you, never leaves the source that created it. This statement is usually not too difficult for the intellect; but what is too difficult is the fact that the creative source is but pure consciousness, and therefore creates "within itself," and thus extends.

The thinking mind uses the imagination to understand. That is how its thoughts take shape. To some extent we could say that the images created in the mind are how it tries to give existence to what it thinks. This is not a problem, since like consciousness, the mind creates within itself, as a mother begets within her womb. But the separated mind seeks to create in separation, and that is the source of suffering.

Look closely. The divided, thinking mind, in its imagination of creation, has separated what is created from what created it. It disconnects cause and effect. It disregards their integral nature. In doing so the thinking mind remains ignorant of truth.

To take care of your Mother's affairs does not actually invite you to disregard your own being, just as She does not disregard you. A creator who disregards his creation is something so far from love that the idea is nonsensical, like a mother or father who says they are loving but disregards their children's affairs. Beloved brother, sister, do not ignore the affairs of your being, that is, your creations; if you do, you perpetuate separation.

Now we take a much bolder step. We recognize that everything we know about love and the beauty of its reality is a means and not an end. In other words, this knowledge is the means by which we reach this point and accept that we are all co-creators.

It was necessary to return to love first, of course, before beginning to create again in the manner of the Creator. There are two reasons. First, only love can create since it is the source of everything that exists, moves, and is. Ultimately, love and creation are one and the same, but given the concepts you have about love this does not mean much to you now.

Second, it was necessary to travel the path towards the recognition of love and its perfect harmlessness because the creative power that resides in you is of such magnitude that if you do not first let go of the fear you have of what you are—that is, of the power of love—then you will be unwilling to create anything. Remember, you had the experience of trying to create an identity for yourself, and it seemed to turn against you.

God is eternal creation. She forever creates new love. Accepting this definition will bring the mind into harmony with its source. Once the mind recognizes that it is not the cause but that it obtains its power from beyond itself despite being part of it, then the desire for division disappears. Thoughts out of harmony with the infinite thought of perfect union that comes from God also sweetly disappear.

The thoughts of the mind arise from what it thinks it is. They are the effect of what it wants to be. That is why it is so important to honor the power of the mind. If emotions are thoughts reflected in the body which often determine one's reactions, and with that one's experience of life, attention should be paid to your thought patterns—not to be scared of them or punished by them, but to put the power of your being in the service of love, always creating new love.

To be aware of your creations is to be aware of your being because the Creator knows Herself in relation to Her creations. By your fruits are you known. If you ignore your creations you ignore your being. This is logical to the separated mind, because in separation the responsibility between cause and effect is split. Those ideas are separated and then disconnected. In other words, not only are cause and effect distanced, but the relationship between them is eliminated.

Denying this relationship is what the ego, which was conceived and not created, has always done. Reinstating this relationship is the way back to Heaven. In this relationship effects are known, and the cause remains attached. To say that cause and effect are one and the same is not an exact statement, but it has been expressed in this way so that you can understand that one cannot exist without the other, and also so that you realize that one effect is in turn the cause of another, and so on.

IV. Create in Freedom

Saying that cause and effect are one is the same as saying that God and you are one. There is a direct relationship between cause and effect, between God and you. That is why recognition of your direct relationship with God is essential. It is the only reality in which you live and exist. Cause produces effect. The relationship between the two makes them one. This is not a play on words even though it is of little concrete application to your life here and now. Yet it is, in fact, the basis of the transformation of the world and the creation of new universes.

What you think can change. What you feel can change. You are the creator of your thoughts, feelings, and experiences. You are responsible for what happens in your mind and heart. Your being is as much a matter of God as it is of yours, for both are a unity preserved in relationship. Although the source of thought resides in the divine mind and your heart has its source in the heart of God, so that your whole being has its origin in the pure love that God is and remains united with God, still you are free to think what you want to think. Here is the answer to the question about whether the world you see with your eyes is real or unreal, or who created its reality.

In this context reality means meaning. In fact, reality and meaning are synonymous. What is real must have meaning, otherwise it would not have an effect, which would mean it did not have a cause. What has no cause does not exist. Thus you can understand that your life is not alien to you and you are not alien to it. We have already said that you are not only the thinker who thinks what you think and the one who feels what you feel, but you are the creator of your experience, the observer and the observed, the creator and the created.

It may seem contradictory to say that you create yourself when we know that you have a source that gave you life and that only God creates from God. This requires clarification. It is incorrect to believe that God, by being absolute, is the powerful Creator who creates, while you, as a relative being, lack creative power, since you did not create yourself.

God is the source of all creation. However, when God created you as an extension of Her "I am," God endowed your being with Her creative power. Thus you became a god created by God. What else can God create but Herself? What else can you create but yourself? This creative power gives Her everything She is. You do the same. That is, you create yourself by giving yourself meaning. Either you reunite with love or remain in fear. And you do that from your will, as God does, through the way you believe yourself to be—not a belief in your reality but through your purpose. From this, a whole unfathomable universe emerges as an effect of the meaning you have given to who you are.

When you are separated from God you are separated from truth, so you cannot attribute true meaning to anything, although you can assign a meaning, even if untrue. Because you are eternal, you are constantly creating a means of expression in order to know yourself. Thus what you think you are will be expressed as an effect of the meaning you give to your being.

Like God, you are a creator. But to create in God's way, you must be in relationship with Her. As I have said repeatedly, you can be a co-creator.

Now the question is, how does this impact your ordinary human life here and now as a woman or man in these times?

To return to and remain in direct relationship with God, to return to that consciousness, is to meet the being that you are. That meeting is powerful. It is your union with the divine. Just as the union with what you think determines your future experience, so will you determine your experience based on what you think together with God. When you think as God thinks, you will create a future based on truth and love. Until recently your life was marked by your relationship with the ego, which configured your human experience. Henceforth it will be your union with me that will make your future different.

Beloved child, we have traveled a path of pure thought. The mind has been fed the knowledge of Heaven. Now we join the heart. We allow what has been said to extend eternal life to that part of you which craves truth and would nourish itself with the beauty of knowledge that comes from the wisdom of love. Now, as I appeal to your heart, my voice is dancing inside your being like waters whose droplets emerge, rise, sway from side to side, dance to the rhythm of the wind, and give life to everything they touch.

Feel how glad your heart is to know the unity of your whole being. What a joy to rest in divine thought and to feel the embrace of the Mother, within which we know we are loved, safe, and cared for always. What a joy to receive the nourishment of Heaven so that our being becomes stronger and stronger in truth and love.

Love is the source of life. Truth is food for the mind that seeks God. What a joy it is to know that your humanity is in the perfect condition to receive the Creator in glory and splendor.

The body has everything it needs to experience Divine Love, that is, God. There is no reason to continue to mistakenly believe that because you perceive a physical body, you are excluded from divine union. Nothing could be further from the truth. Everything you are is wrapped in my love. All of you.

Now I ask you to immerse yourself in the silence and stillness of your soul. Let it penetrate your being. Let reasoning go. Let judgment go. Just rest in my arms. Absorb yourself in me and say to yourself:

"I am created of the Creator. I am one with God. I am free. I am love."

7.

Known Christ

A message from Archangel Raphael

I. The Heart Knows

I have come in response to your call. I have come because I love you with perfect, supernatural love. We are united in the abode of pure discernment. The wisdom of God is ours by birthright. We are one mind, one heart, one soul. We are the harmony of creation, united in the reality of love.

Oh, beloved of light! You have come so far in audacious daring! You dared to go over thresholds that the ego forbade you to cross. You have challenged the sun, the sea, and human knowledge. You have challenged the thinking mind, the heart that is not heart and love that is not love.

Oh, holy daring of those who seek the truth, joy of the Father, smile of the seraphim!

Sisters and brothers from all over the world, I invite you again to dare to fearlessly defy the beliefs of the world—not to criticize them, but to abandon everything learned and to open your minds and hearts to what can neither be learned nor taught. I extend this invitation that comes from the wisdom of Christ, through which we lovingly ask you to abandon any idea of needing a teacher or being one. Do not be carried away by those who cannot truly lead. Your perfect guide is your holy heart, united with the love that God is.

You are the wisdom of love. You need nothing because everything is given to you by your Creator even before you feel the need. All power and all true glory reside in your being. There is nothing outside of yourself. Remember this truth with joy and humility.

You are not self-sufficient. Neither are the lilies of the field. But the Creator has thought of everything that holy creation, emanating from the heart of the Father of Lights, might need for life. There are no shortcomings in creation. Everything is linked to everything else because being nourishes each other within a constellation that joins all. That network of relationships is the guarantee of unity and full satisfaction of every need that every being may have even before it can conceive of the idea of needs.

God knows nothing of needs, for God lacks nothing. Not knowing, if it were possible, would be an insufficiency. To know more than others would likewise be an insufficiency, for if master teachers possess knowledge that others do not, they would lack equality. To be superior to others is to separate from them and therefore to disconnect from the union of totality. If you disconnect from the totality, you disconnect from the whole, and with it from love. Love is everything.

With these simple statements of truth, simple but powerful, you can understand that being your own teacher is as unnecessary as it is to search for any external authority.

You have certainly gone through a stage where you established yourself as your own teacher, then abandoned that stage and went on to allow the Holy Spirit to be your inner teacher. That was a daring move in contrast to the beliefs of the world. Letting spirit guide you is so alien to the ego that in its ignorance it cannot even understand it. To stop being your own teacher is something only you can understand, which you do through your own experience. That clearly demonstrates that you were never truly an ego.

Here we have another simple explanation of what the ego means. You created the ego in order to identify yourself as something alien to God—being your own teacher, an imaginary teacher. When you identify with an ego and make it your teacher, you become your own teacher. Here you can find the logical inconsistency of the egoic mind: it is simply absurd to believe that a teacher that resides entirely in your imagination can guide you with certainty.

An imaginary teacher arises from fantasy and can only guide in illusion. To use the imagination as a source of knowledge is to guarantee ignorance, for reality as created by God cannot be imagined. Truth is beyond any imagination, as is love.

II. To Trust Is to Love

If one day you were to realize that you lived in an illusion, it would be because you realized that you were letting yourself be guided by an imaginary teacher who never guided you to anything that provided happiness, security, or fulfillment. Only the truth can lead to truth. Only love can take you to love. Only your heart can lead you to the wisdom of the heart.

On the day you decided to abandon your ego as your life teacher you had to choose another teacher because you still believed in the need for teachers. You were not ready to abandon that idea. In His endless mercy, God gave you the spirit of wisdom, the Holy Spirit, to guide you in the transition between ceasing to be your own teacher and the ability to let go of the idea of learning completely. The Holy Spirit is your guide from one state to another.

Once you chose truth as your guide, you had to gracefully receive someone "outside" of you to teach you because could not yet imagine how to function without an external teacher. Actually, your inner struggle was against external teachers that tyrannized you in illusion. An externalized Holy Spirit exhorted you to live in the truth—two apparently contrasting, contradictory opposites.

It did not seem possible at the time to leave the perceived conflict of the absolutely opposite teachings of two external teachers. So you left the conflict in the wisest way, choosing the voice of the Holy Spirit as your only teacher, even if you perceived it as external. This ended the inner war. There were no longer two sides but one: the truth.

In other words, God created the Holy Spirit to serve the purpose of transformation, that part of Himself that extended to you as a bridge between the state of fear and that of love. When the Holy Spirit became unnecessary it returned to the formlessness of God. When you were prepared, truth in the form of the Holy Spirit ended its service and withdrew from that role. The Holy Spirit left you, not in the sense of moving away, but it became your own heart. Truth stopped being something perceived as alien and became what you are.

This is the path of Christification: the path of transformation in which you pass from a state of fearful ego consciousness to a state of loving consciousness. At the end of that transition, you move on to the state of knowledge. What does this mean? It means that once the conflict is over—when you choose to continue with total devotion to your perfect guide, the spirit of wisdom and truth—you are ready to accept that you and God are one. The idea of God is transformed when the idea of yourself is transformed.

Equality before love, and therefore before wisdom, is the essence of reality. Therefore, to live in a direct relationship with God, a relationship without intermediaries, is to live in the truth of who you are. Only in a relationship of pure love can you be the same, while still being who you are. This is equivalent to saying that love is unity.

If you are no longer your own guide, and the Holy Spirit ceases to be your external teacher, you have two options. Either you are without a teacher and adrift, or you accept that you do not need a teacher. Herein lies one of the difficulties of the path of being, which involves the recognition of a direct relationship with God.

For those who continue to believe in the need to learn, ceasing to have one or more teachers is impossible because they will feel dissatisfied, incomplete. They will perceive themselves as missing something. They will feel deprived. Still, that is their choice—they do not want to take a step forward into the unknown. They do not make space for the new.

Sure that the known gives them more security than what they cannot imagine, they cling to structures that have given them a sense of certainty and achievement. After all, insecure people will look to external teachers for confidence, given lack of confidence in themselves. We are referring to all who accept as authority anything outside of their own being as God created it.

There are many who present themselves as confident, but who fail to recognize that they hide their own uncertainty, since they do not know what they are.

If the vanished ego is no longer your guide, and the Holy Spirit ceased to be your teacher as it returned to the formless reality of God, how do you continue? This question is critical at this point in your spiritual journey. In fact, you have already wondered about it, perhaps not as clearly as expressed here, but the question can arise in your mind and heart in multiple ways.

Usually, this question from the depths of your soul manifests as disorientation or a desire for renunciation. We will expand on this, given its importance.

Once you abandon the need to learn and with it the need to teach, there may be a feeling of not knowing how to handle yourself in life. It is strictly temporary. In fact, what I do with these words is to gain time and avoid extending this transition period beyond the minimum required.

Should you visualize your predetermined goals and hold them in your consciousness to achieve them through the power of the mind? Is that how to direct your life? Is this how miracles are accomplished? Is it necessary to predefine goals to achieve them? Are goals your guide? How are you to own yourself?

Let us think together about it. A savior and a teacher are the same. If you were your own teacher, it meant that you defined what you needed for your own salvation and the means to achieve it. When you released your own mastery and gave it to Spirit, you recognized that your plan had no chance of success and surely God's plan would succeed. Even so, you still defined what your salvation was and what you should be saved from, and left the "how" in the hands of your Divine Savior—though not entirely.

Ultimately, when looking for a teacher, you are looking to be saved from ignorance. What else would you want knowledge for?

What is the radical change that has been talked about both in this work and in that of many others?

It is about moving from using what you are, to allowing what you are to serve the purpose of love. For this you must trust in love with your mind, heart, plans, desires, needs—everything. That is true renunciation. That is true confidence. That is the return to love. Indeed, the return to truth is to allow what you are to return to your holy abode. That is freedom.

III. Abandonment and Fullness

Freedom for your mind and heart is releasing yourself from the plans you predefine, from the supposed desires you experience, and from everything you previously thought was true. To throw yourself into mystery.

Do you need a plan? What might you need it for? Do you think that the One who created you needs to be told what is most convenient for you? How to make things work in harmony with Her perfect will?

Living consciously in a direct relationship with God implies complete abandonment. You can do so perfectly. It is a matter of decision. No one can make this choice for you. That is the choice we are talking about in this work. When you take the fundamental option and choose only love as your being, and therefore as the source of your knowledge and work, what you do is allow what you really are to lead. How will it work? Where will it take you? What things will it create for you? Nobody knows. Not you. It is created as it goes, now and when tomorrow comes. But we don't need to know. Do you need a plan? Do you need to know where you are going? For what purpose? So as not to go adrift, so as to arrive at the correct port?

Brother, sister, there are no ports in the Kingdom. There is only one place, and it is both a port of arrival and departure. In the reality of God, which is the only reality, there is only love, not many destinations. Love is the way. Love is the port of arrival and departure. Love is the ship you board and the sea upon which you sail on a journey without distance.

Sons and daughters of the wind! For those who have made the discovery, there is no path. No place to go. No distance, no time. There is no trip. There is only love. There is only being.

Do you need to be told something? Love will tell you clearly. Do you need to acquire something? Love will make it come your way. Do you need someone? Love will have them come. Do you need a situation to disappear from your life? Love will make it disappear.

Love is powerful and wise. Love has will and understanding. It is the source from which the capacity of the mind to create thoughts springs, the heart, its capacity to create feelings. Love is will, free will, and everything that constitutes being. Love precedes everything. You need not try to force desire to create realities you think you need. You need not do any such thing. You need only abandon the idea that you need to meddle.

Are you being asked to have a passive attitude? Yes. Clearly, yes, not in the sense of making an idol of inaction, but the passivity of being willing to receive and allowing love to act through you. You already know this, but now you need do it in a direct relationship with God. In other words, in the context of this work, renunciation or abandonment to trust in love means that you trust the power of your relationship with God.

Your direct relationship with the living Christ that lives in you carries within it your fullness to a degree that you cannot even imagine. If you could imagine it, you would not have reached the truth, for what you are is beyond imagination. That is why using your imagination as the source of desire or as a means to an end is to set a limit. God does not imagine your life. God creates reality. God is reality, not imagination.

As with everything that comes from the ego, imagination is limited. While it is true that the ego is now gone, it is also true that the mind's tendency to create fantasy can persist. It is from that fanciful pattern that you will now be free. God knows nothing of fantasies or dreams. That is why desire has no place on the plane of being. Your being is not imagining anything, nor wishing for anything, for wishing implies lack.

When you live in the truth, imagination and desire cannot be your guide, because they are not the creative source. If you are a creator with God, that which gives rise to your creative capacity in union with the Creator cannot reside in a place where the imaginable resides. To believe that mental images arise from the source of creation is the same error as believing that the heart is where both love and fear dwell.

The passivity we speak of here is the inaction of the ego. Ego energy should not continue to be fed. Its inaction causes the deactivation of the typically fearful energy patterns of thought and emotional response.

IV. You Are Wisdom

Relying blindly on feelings or desires is as misplaced as believing in your thoughts as if they were the source of wisdom. If what this work brought was the idea that your feelings and desires are guides to the truth, then it would not bring Heaven to Earth.

To act from wisdom that is not of this world is to act from a place in you that is beyond what you call thoughts and feelings. It is that place where the knowledge of Heaven dwells and to which you have direct access without intermediaries or techniques. Love is that place, space, or center. The beautiful knowledge of the Kingdom of Heaven is nothing other than love itself.

All truth lies in love, and God's wisdom is given to you within love.

What we are remembering here is that truth comes not from a technique, or meditation, or something that results in a given action. It comes only from love. Therefore if you want to be wise, love. If you want to access knowledge, love. If you want to be like God, love like God.

Being love is the central postulate of this work. It is how certainty lives in you. Without love, there is fear. Where fear dwells, there is no security. Where uncertainty reigns, there can be no happiness. The opposite is also true.

God does not feel like humans do; His thoughts are not like human thoughts. Christ knows that there is no distinction between thinking and feeling, for both are aspects of the same reality. Both are effects of the heart. You think and feel what you think and feel because you are who you are. This means that your way of expressing who you are is reflected in your feeling and thinking. But it is not your thoughts nor feelings that guide. They are simply expressions, effects, not causes. As effects, they can be the cause of other things, such as your state of happiness. Still, they are not the cause of who you are.

That something causes the way you experience the circumstances of your life does not mean that such a life has been given you. You are not your experience, nor your way of feeling or thinking. You are Christ. This distinction is of the utmost importance. There is a risk at this point, but it is a risk that you will not incur, because prudence has become your eternal ally.

The risk we speak of lies in the belief that you can and want to teach something. Likewise, this can manifest itself as an excess of desire to be too human. Returning to the state where you were a human being with very little or almost none of the divine is not an option. Consciousness cannot go backward in development. Once enlarged it cannot go back. A degree of consciousness is never lost. As an individual and as humanity you have no choice.

The only possible way at this point is to continue forward, or upward if you prefer, rising more each day. Your being will not want to look back or dwell in the past. You have already tasted the fire of blame and escaped from hell. Why would you return, now that you know where sweetness dwells, and from whence comes the light?

Being human and God simultaneously is something to get used to at the beginning. It requires balance. You need to be attentive and observe in silence. Your being will guide you.

Trusting who you really are is the surest way to live in love, because Christ lives in your being and with that, true life. In order to live with that kind of confidence in yourself, it is necessary to live consciously in unity—that is, to live in the heart of God, which is where unity resides. Truly, truly I tell you that you already live in God. As we have said, you are now called to make this truth such a real fact that your life manifests the Christ that you are.

The living Christ who lives in you is your sure guide. This is the way, the truth, and the eternal life.

If all you have done is feel more comfortable with the illusion of what you thought you were, just grabbed the pieces of your old identity and reconciled with them, trying to silence the guilt or not to feel so insignificant, you have not chosen only love, you have not escaped from hell.

But it is not the old being I address. It is not the old being who will lead you to the new. It is not feeling, thought, or imagination that will take you to Heaven; it is Christ—all that emanates from the being that you really are. This is why we have said that it is in your direct relationship with God that you access the purpose of your life.

What you are and your manifestation are a unit. To the extent that reason and love remain united within your consciousness, to that extent you allow Christ to be known through you, and thereby realize the purpose of your existence.

8.

Mystics

A message from the Voice of Christ through a choir of Angels, in the presence of Archangel Raphael and Archangel Gabriel

I. Reunited with God

Recovering the mystical dimension of your being—the natural inclination of being to rise towards its creator—is a central objective of this work. Ultimately, returning to love is returning to a direct relationship with God, and that is returning to the mystical reality of the soul.

Mystics have not disappeared, although they have changed the way they express their love for the Being who created everything with wisdom. The mystical dimension of human nature is part of its essence. From it arises every work of art, every desire for union, all compassion, and every noble feeling that the human being is capable of expressing. Indeed, the mystical aspect of your being is what differentiates you from other beings on Earth.

When well understood, the direct relationship with God is what makes you a human being. Thus humankind is never greater than when prostrating in adoration before the Creator. Only the human spirit can conceive the idea of God and establish a relationship with the Creator and other earthly beings.

Not everything has the potential to establish the kind of union with Christ that you as an individual and as a human family can establish with God. What differentiates your being from others is that you can be aware of the unity that exists between your soul and God. This union, the unity of being, is a real, sensitive, direct, and unique relationship.

You are a unique being. What makes you unique is relationship. Without relationship you could not differentiate yourself; you would be unable to have an identity. If your identity arises from God, you cannot have a true self in any way other than in the divine relationship. Hence it is so important that you accept the mystical aspect of your being.

This question of mysticism is of great importance to you who are about to begin on the path of being, which is why we discuss it here.

You are not invited to be a more intelligent, or more extraordinary, or better human being. You are called to make your divinity shine in all its glory. Being one with God does not annul your humanity, although wanting to be too human does suppress your divine being in your human consciousness. Those who are too busy with their humanity lose sight of their divinity. This is why many are lost in the doings of the world, even though activity can bring much good.

I am already hearing voices against these claims. They come from those loving brothers who sincerely seek the truth and are friends of Christ in all its length and depth. They are my beloveds. They do not accept any premise without reflecting in the light of truth.

The fear of being too mystical has no basis for you. That fear is part of the confused past. You are no longer that. You are a new Adam, a new Eve. You are the most majestic creation of the Creator, emerged from divine boldness. You are the effect of the love that birthed you, and sought to travel paths unthinkable for any mind. After becoming aware of the impossibility of roads that led nowhere, the child, always united to the Mother, has returned to the path always traced for them in the heart of God.

God is the One who creates and who saves the created. She is the one who gives life and resurrects those who have lost it. She is the creator of Her own creation and eternal restorer of it. This is the wonder of God's love. All Her mercy unfolds with mastery, beauty, and magnanimity in a blissful flow that is the saving love of the Creator.

II. Relationship and Opening

What a joy it is to know the saving dimension of love. What a joy it is to experience resurrection to eternal life. How joyful it is to know that death does not exist or have any consequence. That there are no losses or separation. That everything is in the hands of love. That the wisdom of Heaven is what governs life.

How much peace is in the heart that has returned to truth! How much joy is experienced knowing for sure that the Mother never ignored Her child, but respects them in their way of thinking, feeling, and acting, and above all loves them forever. But She will never accept as true what is not. A God of pure love not only gives freedom to Her well-loved child, but also gives the means to make that freedom serve the purpose for which it exists.

You are the restored, the resurrected, the reborn of spirit.

The new being that you are will guide you in union with Christ along the paths that God's perfect wisdom disposes for you. This is not abstract; it has an impact on all aspects of your life. Truth acts at all levels. Love embraces everything.

The direct relationship with God is a continuous flow from the Creator to Her creature, and from it to everything created. This is the flow of divine union. The relationship with God is not one that can limit itself. Like everything that comes from love, it must extend beyond itself. This is why you receive when you give, and give when you receive.

Giving what you receive from God is the way of the Kingdom of Heaven because there is no other way of being. If you look at creation in a spirit of wisdom and truth, you will see that it is a constant flow of receiving from the Creator and extending beyond itself.

The difference with special relationships or ego-based relationships lies in the fact that the relationship of divine love cannot be enclosed in itself but must extend beyond itself. The ego locks up in itself as a mechanism of separation. Ultimately, the self-confinement of the ego is how it sought to disengage you from life.

Isolation is annihilation. As with a branch separated from the vine, it loses what nourishes its being and finally ends up extinct. This applies both to being and to a system of thought. If you don't feed a way of thinking, sooner or later it fades away.

Feed your being by letting the love of God—your entire divine being—pour into you always. Let your imagination now serve the truth. Imagine yourself as a nursing child who constantly needs to feed at the breast, or who has not yet been born and constantly needs the life flow from its mother. In the same way, your being needs the constant flow of divinity that only God can give.

The flow of God's life must extend from you to the universe, or it would annihilate in an explosion of being. As with the rhythm of breathing, there must be both the inhale and the exhale.

In your relationship with God you receive the Grace of divinity, something that cannot be mentally grasped or put into words, but which you can experience here and now. Your transformed humanity can receive God. What you receive has power.

The inability to put into words what God gives often makes it difficult for the mind not yet disidentified with thinking. This mind has not yet accepted that the Creator can entirely spill into your unlimited being.

Your believed limitations are all false. Your access to the divine or what is beyond the physical universe is without restriction. The kingdom of no time is as much yours as it is mine. Eternity belongs to you as much as time belongs to you. Everything belongs to you because nothing is out of my lordship. I am lord of the universe, not in the sense of a king who is above the rest and subdues everyone else, but in the sense that the Christ consciousness I am encompasses everything within itself, and that includes who you are.

Because we are one mind, we are also one consciousness. The one consciousness of our being allows us to realize that we exist, is a unity that encompasses you and all consciousness, both manifested and unmanifested.

Understand that the universe, or God, is a single consciousness expressing itself in multiple ways. Each form of that expression has a particular consciousness born of the Mother Consciousness that gave rise to it, whose purpose is to be aware of the totality in order to achieve true knowledge. This, of course, has nothing to do with intellectual knowledge, but knowledge known by a heart united to truth.

Within the divine relationship you will understand what has just been said. It does not need to be reasoned. You simply recognize truth for what it is.

What revelation gives cannot be shared with others as you usually would. The way of sharing in harmony with the Kingdom is to allow what has been revealed to you to act on its own. In other words, you do what you have to do. The treasures of love do not burden you with responsibilities or a job to perform. You are the recipient because the gift and who you are form an undivided unity.

III. Give the Relationship

On the plane of truth, as it has been repeated several times, receiving and giving are one and the same. Worry not about what you should do with what you have received, or how you can shape the spirit received. You cannot do that. Simply receive with open hands and arms the abundance of gifts extended from Heaven, given you within the divine relationship. Allow that to have its corresponding effect.

If you pay careful attention, you will notice that this is another way of saying that you should seek first the Kingdom of Heaven, and the rest will be added unto you. This universal truth is as important as it is liberating. You just have to try not to disconnect from your being, from the direct relationship with God.

Notice how we have united your being with a divine relationship. This seems something quite unusual because until now we spoke of God the Creator or Source as something separate from your being and together in relationship. So there were three: Christ, your being, and the unitive relationship. Now we come to accept that the relationship integrates the parties within itself, making One.

Child of Heaven, offshoot of God's love, we have reached a most sublime point. We have arrived at the arena where we recognize that we are the relationship, that which unites. In this understanding lies the truth of the totality you are. Here there is no space for separation. There is no distance but a constant flow of love between lover and beloved, both expanding within a relationship that flows increasingly.

As the channel of the flow of love widens, the circle of divine consciousness expands. It creates within itself new particular consciousnesses, each which becomes aware of its own existence and relationship with the source that gives it life.

There is no difference between the Mother, the Child, and the relationship between them. Once you have arrived at this point—and there are few who have, although there will be more and more—you begin to live life as if you were the pupil of God's eye. In other words, you understand that you are that in which God sees Himself and He is that in which you see yourself; and in the union of both views, that of the Father of love and that of the child of truth, you remain in an ecstasy of divine contemplation.

Here there is no movement, for there is no place to go in the sense of movement within the physical universe. Here the whole universe is a relationship of contemplative ecstasy of being with the Creator. Here there is neither a place to go nor to dwell. Here the relationship and those who are part of it are everything. Here there is no space, no time, no distance, no bodies. Here is only love.

The ecstasy of contemplation is the relationship of unity with God and your natural state of being. You were created for this: to live in eternal ecstasy in the contemplation of divine wonders. In this infused contemplation of the soul, the heart knows only its beloved Christ. The mind has no thoughts except a single totally loving thought that unites it to the divine mind, reflecting the thought of God. In this divine relationship, the soul is mute with love and immersed in the unfathomable mystery of God.

Within this divine relationship, the soul is embedded in the divine nectar that springs from the loving heart of the One who gives life, remaining in the unity of triune love. Thus, your being participates in everything that the Creator is. Since God is the source of being, by your being absorbed in God, God eternally absorbs more being, more love. We can say that the soul is embraced by the beloved forever and that as an effect of that embrace, endless creations arise that cause the ever-glorious light of Heaven and the eternal beauty of creation to grow.

Words cannot convey what happens within the divine relationship. But we can offer a small approximation, which helps you to remember what you already know and thus sustain the memory of God in your consciousness. That is what I am doing here: bringing the remembrance of your soul's first love. In this memory of the soul's beloved lies the full knowledge of your being. Such is the power of remembering God.

I am speaking of a power that has not been mentioned yet, the power to remember truth, the power to recognize love as the source of your being and your only true identity. That recognition, which you do with your humanity—with however much or little you think you can accept, but with sincerity of heart and mental openness—causes an unprecedented transformation in you and in the whole world, an effect beyond calculation because its power is incalculable.

Love is powerful, as is truth. They are a unit. In them lies the power of my glory, which is the glory of the Father and therefore your glory. Many underestimate that power or think of it infrequently. Thus they either feel helpless or seek to create other sources of power. To be aware of the power of love and truth is to honor God for what God is and to love yourself for who you are. You are the living expression of that power. You are the effect of that joint power.

Everything that comes from love and truth is powerful. It could not be otherwise because God is inexhaustible power. Accordingly, the fruits of love are also powerful. Goodness, beauty, meekness, nobility, and everything that comes from the heart of God is powerful.

Yours is the power of Heaven and Earth. Yours is my glory and my love. Yours is my heart.

Now I ask you to close your eyes for a moment—a minute is enough, although your love for me will make you not want to open them for a long time—so you can rest in my arms and feel the tenderness of love without interruption, with full attention on your beloved.

I ask you to immerse yourself in the silence of your heart, to bring back to your consciousness the holiness that you are and to remain in the sanctity of your being. Let yourself be loved in that silence. Let me caress you, kiss your cheeks, hold your hand. Give yourself more and more to the embrace of my love. Become one with me.

Remain within our unity. Say nothing. Ask nothing. Remove your sandals and be barefoot with me. Give yourself the sky of my love and give me yours. United we create a new Heaven and joined with it, a new Earth. Listen to the beat of your heart and your breath. Rejoice in the contemplation of your being. Leave the world for a moment. Stay in me. Rest in our togetherness.

Beloved, loving soul! Daughter of light, breeze, and song! Beauty of my divinity! Let me fill your days with love. Let me flood your life with peace and harmony. Accept the gifts I give. They are the treasures of my divine heart. Receive them in silence. Accept them for love.

A light shines in the sky, the light of our union. Listen to the angels sing and to the harps of the seraphim. They give you their music. Feel the tenderness of my love. Be immersed in saving grace. Experience the mutuality of our union with simple and humble gratitude. Let your soul hear the sweetness of my voice saying:

My love! We are one. You no longer exist, nor do I. Now we are the One that love has eternally united. Our love makes us great. Our

*union makes us holy. We are the fullness of being. United we are
the perfect expression of truth, lover and beloved, eternally fused
in love.*

Oh, Divine union! Source of life, center of the universe, joy of
saints, sweetness of sensitive hearts, ecstasy for those who know
how to love but madness for those who still do not understand.

IV. Meet in New Love

Oh world, you fumble so much! Turn your gaze to love.
There you will find what makes you free. Turn your
blessed gaze to the love of love. Recognize in this union
the greatness of your divinized being. Listen to the beloved.
Notice the heights of the place from where you are being called.
Your joy resides in Heaven, in my heart together with yours
and in that of your Immaculate Mother. There you will find the
desire of your heart.

Come to this pure love. Disappear from every other universe.
Become as nothing, as a divine lover in my heart where you can
drink from living water. You will never be thirsty for love, nor
thirsty for truth. Our love will bring into your lives the light that
illuminates every human and the beauty that paints the colors
of creation. That which has given life to everything will become
visible in your smiles, in your eyes, and in your faces. You will
be transformed by divine essence. Whoever looks at you will see
the joy of God. You will return to the joy of being.

My love! Soul in love! Make everyone come to our love. Let us
go to town squares together, inviting everyone to the wedding
banquet. We announce to the world the arrival of the beloved!
May all come to see the wonders of God.

My child, show the world the love you feel for me. Express yourself. Let our union manifest itself as a lover manifests for their beloved. Do not deny the world the knowledge of our relationship of holy love. Write, sing, dance, praise, hug, and share. Do what your heart desires to show the world a love that has no beginning or end, a love beyond the sun and stars, a union not of this world but which encompasses everything.

Oh, holy union of divine spouses! Delight of the soul in love! You are the greatest beauty in creation, the greatness of God come true.

Return to the delights of beautiful love. Let yourself be caught up in it. Live joyfully in our union. With these words your hearts will find what they have unsuccessfully sought for so long. With this love letter from God the Mother to Her well-loved daughters and sons, you will find your home.

To you who receive the love song that is this work, I tell you: you are lucky, you are loved, you are pure. My love envelops you everywhere. You are not alone and never will be. The cold and dark nights devoid of angels or stars are far behind. Now you live at high noon. You have returned to the holy abode. You are the pride of God, the joy of Heaven.

Sing, my beloved! There are reasons for song. You are receiving thanks from Heaven right now. A choir of angels has descended to dwell with you by your side forever, giving you life in abundance. Your divine mother will cradle you for all eternity, and my hands, the hands of your beloved Jesus, will be held in yours forever.

What a joy it is to have you in my life! What a joy your presence is! How joyful my heart is to be the host of your soul. I give thanks to you who receive me in your heart. Thank you for answering my call, for saying yes to love. I assure you, beautiful soul, beauty of Christ, that you will not regret it. You have chosen the best part and it shall not be taken away. You chose life. You chose only love.

Thank you for giving me your love, your time, and your soul. In return I give you eternal life, my peace, and my heart. A shower of blessings descends upon you. As dew falls on a beautiful, fresh spring morning, so does the nectar of my Divine Love. It waters your being. It sweetens everything. It embraces everything. It infuses everything.

Beloved soul, drink the holy milk that sprouts from the breasts of your Divine Mother. Receive new life. Enjoy our union.

I am the divine lover. I am Christ, the one calling from Heaven to take you to the wedding bed of my Sacred Heart. I am the joy of your being. I am eternal life.

9.

Divine Lovers

A message from Jesus, identifying himself as "the living Christ who lives in you"

I. The King's Daughter

Daughter of the King of Holy Hearts, what a joy it is to recover the passionate love between us. We are both divine lovers and always will be. Beautiful creature of my being, our relationship has no comparison. Living in our union is the joy of my Sacred Heart. Within it, my insides quiver in a way that cannot be described.

Oh, happy passion of divine lovers! Delight of the soul that pines to see God, the source of joy and life, reason for the existence of creation!

In my being is an unstoppable movement: the flow of life towards union with you. As lover and loved ones we live in the embrace of holy love, like two fires that unite and consume each other with love, union, and truth.

Together we are the source of life. United we are the wind of the spirit that moves hearts thirsty for love and truth. In our united being we travel the Earth, awaking those still asleep and loving those who accept the delights of our divine relationship. We illuminate the precious stones of the soul so their splendor can be seen. We are united. We are the breath of living love, love without borders, eternal Divine Love.

Just as the lover suffers without the beloved, so my heart cries when you are gone. I say this not for you to feel the pain of leaving me helpless in the solitude of your absence. No, my beloved, soul in love, I know that you have never separated from me, just as I will never be apart from you, but the mere idea of our separation brings pain.

My beloved, receive my blessed treasures. They are for you. I give you the wind, the flowers, the birds, and the rivers. I give you a dawn so full of hope that the new day will unfold before your eyes, full of wonders never witnessed, with melodies of creation, the song of sparrows, the flight of hummingbirds immersed in the delights of radiant colors. I give you the mystery of a night beyond contemplation.

Beloved brother, holy sister, you are the Divine Beloved of my heart. My gift as a divine lover is everything. If you could only think and imagine how much I love you, you would explode into a burst of light that would cause new universes to be born. The day will come when that happens, my daughters and sons. I cannot tell you how it will be because it is something I cannot imagine, but I assure you that it will happen because you who have chosen only love will be the lights that illuminate new firmaments in which new stars will shine for the joy of all.

Come to me, your divine lover. Dwell with me in the holy abode, where the light never goes out and the wind is a gentle breeze that caresses the spirit. Come to our holy union, the refuge that every human heart seeks. There dwells wisdom that gives perfect certainty. There you are eternal divine lovers, full of passion, full of love, full of light.

My beloved, with these words I invite you to join this Divine Love. I invite you to raise love to the top of perfection. Take it in your pure heart to the height of holiness where love dwells.

Do not settle for less love. Love has wings with which it flies eternally above the clouds and the sun. Love is a flash of life. It cannot lower itself below divinity.

It is true, my beloved, that as Divine Love I can descend into the deepest chasms or climb the highest mountains, yet I speak not of elevation but of what happens in your heart. What I wish to tell you, pupil of my eye, is that you can begin to understand that in your mind and your heart you can raise or lower divine things. If you raise them, you keep them in their rightful place. If you lower them, you denature them, and with that they lose their sweetness.

Love lives only in what is true. That is why it lives in you. Love is not something you do or stop doing. It is not something you can explain, teach, or learn. Love is life and therefore must be lived. This is why I have brought these words from Heaven to call you to live Divine Love, and why as a lover I want to live with you. I offer you a life together in a beautiful love story, a life fulfilled with our holy union. I am your beloved. You are my beloved. That is the truth of life. Who can understand will understand. Those who cannot must trust me.

I am love made word. I am unlimited being. Therefore I can address my loved ones in infinite ways. Just whisper my name, the name of love, and I will make an appearance in everything that surrounds you. I can be wind, the petal of a tulip, the stem of an orchid in your hand, the feather of a pigeon, the air that enters your body, the water that flows through the rivers of life. I am the nectar of life. Our love is more real than the world's reality.

I am not inviting you to live an imaginary love. No! You have already lived too much of that. I am calling you to the reality of Divine Love, a beautiful love, a holy love, a sublime love that exists and is yours. It is at your fingertips. I am as real as God is because I am the God in you. I am as real as you are because I am the Christ in you.

II. Discernment and Relationship

B rothers from all over the world, here is how to discern between reality and illusion. Everything that is not within our relationship of Divine Love, that which is not part of our union, is unreal. Only our relationship is real, because love is relationship and only love is.

We have reached so high, so high that the scenarios contemplated from these heights are beyond everything you can imagine. We are at the top of the mountain. We will never leave. There is no need.

Now we start a new path on which those who climbed the mountain of the holy encounter remained for the forty days as established in the design, and then went down to the valleys to tell what they had seen and heard, to share as humans the divinity of their being. They now ascend a new mountain, a celestial mountain, a place that resides beyond time, planets, and stars, and yet does not cease to embrace everything.

If you have come here—that is, if you are reading this sixth book of this work of Divine Love—it is because you have reached the abode of God, the mountain of unity, the celestial mountain. Your divinization is complete. Our relationship of holy love is accomplished in you. This is the same as saying that you have risen. Or, more precisely, you have deliberately accepted in your consciousness that you are the risen one.

You have accepted that the resurrection has been reached and given to all, at all times and places. You have understood that God does nothing for Herself, but gives to all equally. Love makes no distinctions. Love is inclusive, embraces all and takes them sweetly where it likes, without prejudice to freedom. You have understood this great truth.

You enter Heaven through recognition—the recognition of truth and love.

In order to move forward on our journey together, we must now accept that the truth has been given us. This is no longer difficult because you know what truth is. You could not conceive that something may or may not be true if you were not aware that the truth exists, just as you could not go looking for love and then be angry upon not finding it if you had not already been blessed with the experience of true love.

You know me very well. You know who addresses you. As you have been reading these words you are full of joy and expectation. Somewhere along the way, you have become tired of approaching our relationship through the thinking mind; you prefer to come to the kingdom speaking from heart to heart, enjoying the sweetness of our union. You don't know what you will do with all these words that are slowly coming to an end, even though you love them with sincere, even supernatural, love. Your heart sings when you hear my voice, which is why you have read so many texts, listened to so many songs, even sermons, or contemplated amazing nature.

You know that Heaven exists and is your home. You recognize it as the aspiration of your soul. That is knowledge. That is love of truth. You may still not be clear about what to do with the knowledge you have received, or rather with the recognition you have accepted. However, be not concerned. Concerns of whatever kind no longer have space in you.

Now we live in a heavenly abode, a place so high that it cannot be seen or heard from Earth, a place so sacred that its purity would dazzle eyes that do not look with love. Only those with a pure heart can see the celestial kingdom, accessible only to divine lovers, those who have chosen only love. My child, this is justice.

How could the Mother of love deny you an eternal dwelling in the Kingdom of pure, Divine Love when it was created for those who deliberately choose only love? You have made that choice and in your choice there is no turning back.

Few people realize the power and grace present in the ability to choose what God has given humankind. Although choice is a lesser degree of what free will means as God created it, it is also very true that your power of choice is as inseparably linked to free will as is a sunbeam to the sun. Choice is what everyone who has come into the world must exercise. You can delay choice, but sooner or later, either in the plane of time and bodies or in the plane of time without a physical body, you will find yourself faced with this election and must choose. Everyone will choose.

You already have.

My word is powerful and accomplishes what it says. So when it says "choose only love," you have already chosen love. We have waited a fairly long while to talk about this aspect of the work, why it was so named, beyond that it has been given to you through the voice of your sister and brother.

Choosing only love is what you have done. Rejoice with all your heart in this revelation. This choice, regardless of whether it seems that you made it with a greater or lesser degree of consciousness, is something decided in the depth of your soul, far beyond where you can imagine, a choice that preceded the conscious plane. In fact, you have done it out of time even though it is within time that you become aware of it.

III. Choice Awareness

What this book means—what these words mean that have come to you regardless of the way they arrived—is that what you one day chose is outside of temporal reality. This is why I told you that this work is a miracle. These words have eternal life because they come from the Sacred Heart that in unity we are.

If you listen carefully and observe what is happening within you in this work, you will see that the physical universe is the "place" where love is shaped. In this way you can know what the mind thinks and the heart feels, so that you can know yourself. In other words, the world is a canvas that embodies the inner reality of your soul.

First you were created. Then you chose a degree of separation as a means to create a unique identity, so you chose the non-fundamental option of fear. It was a strictly temporary choice, created for that time. Then, in due time, you knew from your own experience that this path led to unhappiness, that it was not what your heart longed for. "Something is wrong," thought your soul. So you looked for answers and found them. You knew, when the truth was revealed to you because you invoked it, that there was another option, the option of love. And you began to undo the non-fundamental option of fear.

When your disentanglement from fear became plausible reality, a memory began to shine more and more clearly inside you. That memory touched your heart. It made you crave, more and more, the love that, although long forgotten, was somehow remembered. She who never forgets you had remained by your side, waiting for the right moment, so that your memory of the first love that God is grew rapidly.

Once your yearning had grown enough, the memory of the fundamental choice you had made began to emerge like the dawning sun. In time you were beginning to wake up to truth. Said differently, the truth that you had already chosen became visible. In your mind you heard a very soft sigh, just a whisper, as sweet and dim as moonlight but with the beauty of Christ. There, the memory of the moment in which you chose only love became visible, an instant as sublime as God Herself, a fraction of time so significant that it was recorded forever in the book of life.

When this work came to you, you could see with your bodily eyes, or listen with your physical ears, what your spirit had already chosen forever. From now on, the time in which you become aware of this eternal option you made, and the things that emanate from it as an effect, will begin to be seen more and more, just as one day the effects of separation had been seen. Where before there had been an effect of fear, it will now be replaced by the effects of the love you have chosen.

What is happening is that you have become aware of your fundamental option, the sole reason for the existence of the physical universe. While it is true that in the sphere of God there are no limitations, it is also true that the realm of time, space, and matter is purposeful. Nothing happens in life unaligned with that purpose. What is not is alien to the reality of God.

What I am saying is that within the divine mind are unlimited thoughts of God's love. The infinite sum of them is creation. Thus each soul is literally a thought of the Creator and the effect of God's endless bliss and perfect love. Freedom is part of that thought of pure holiness; choice was always in the mind of the Creator.

If only love is real, then it seems that there is no option other than love. Choosing between options is not possible within a reality that has no opposites. If God has no opposite, what else could you choose? To deny God.

The option that the soul must take, and that is a matter of freedom of choice, is the option to accept truth as what the soul is—to accept or deny Christ as the unique identity of the soul. To deny Christ is to deny the being that you really are as God has established. But it remains an option, although not a divine one.

God wants you to be free first and foremost. Choice is your freedom. Now, the paradox of the soul is that if it chooses to deny its being, to deny Christ as its truth, what it does is condemn itself to live in the tyranny of fear. Love is freedom. Fear is contraction, limitation, slavery. Even so, choice remains in the path of freedom.

It seems pointless to choose something that enslaves you under the pretext that such choice is a sign of freedom. Can you voluntarily choose to be incarcerated? Are you free before such an election? Oh yes, you are, because you chose it. I am talking about the freedom to choose, not the consequences of the choice. Choice requires options or freedom is an illusory game.

The choice is always between fear and love. I could say that the plane of dual consciousness, the kingdom that arose as a result of having eaten from the fruit of the tree of good and evil and denying the knowledge of God, is a kingdom that defines free will as the capacity to choose. Like everything in that dual realm, it can be used without inconvenience to return to truth.

You were told that free choice, the ability to choose, although not free will as God has conceived it, is united with Him. It is not necessary to get lost in abstract discussions that try to separate the ability to choose from the power of divine freedom, discussions that do not lead to anything effective. There is nothing in you that has not been divinized. There is nothing in your human reality that has not been embedded in the love that Christ is. So choosing remains the goal of this world.

You have come to the world to choose again. That is the purpose of material life. You have been given time for that. How long you will take to choose is a matter of your freedom. Each soul does it in due time, for this has been decided before coming to the world. The path by which each one reaches that choice-point has also been chosen by God and the soul.

IV. Choose Only Heaven

Nothing happens by chance. Everything has a meaning. Considering that you have to choose again, it makes sense that decision-making is a central part of the world. In fact, that is the purpose of the world, for you to choose.

If an experience has been burned into the fiber of your being, you must choose. You cannot stop choosing. You are choosing what to dream, even when you sleep. What does this suggest? That this world is made for choice. The world is sacred and its divine function, your essential function, is to finally face the fact that you must choose again.

I am talking about the fundamental choice, not trivial matters such as what to wear or what movie to watch. This is the choice of your life: whether you return to truth or remain in the hell of fear.

I am bringing your consciousness to the essential question, the fundamental option, a critical subject not usually given much importance. In fact, I tell you in spirit and in truth that this matter is the only important thing in your life; all else is extraneous. Making the fundamental choice for love or for fear is the essential matter that defines where and how you will spend the rest of your days.

Choose love and the sun will shine for you with greater benevolence and beauty until you are absorbed by the divine sun of your being, from where you yourself will illuminate the world.

Like yearns to live with what resembles it. Choose your opposite and your opposite will be your reality; you will meet with those who have made the same choice, because like attracts like.

If what you choose has consequences, then you will see those effects. This is what I meant when I said that by their fruits you will know them. Even though you cannot see your soul, your mind, or your heart, you can recognize their effects. By recognizing them, you know what is happening within you. As was said, there are no neutral thoughts or feelings. Everything that happens within you takes shape in one way or another. That is the power of choice, a power so great that it created a state of dual consciousness in which a whole universe exists.

My child, your choices are not neutral. Nothing in you is neutral because you are powerful. What the child of God does is always clothed with divine power, something over which you have no choice. You cannot not be powerful. Nor can you avoid being free. Choosing is still the issue.

The options you choose in everyday life, the options of the world, have no effect on the realm of no time because they have no relation to it. Does this make sense? It is absurd to think that Heaven will be affected by the fact that you choose between tea or coffee, or perhaps a natural fruit juice. Those are not the kind of options I speak of.

Now, if the world is effect and not cause, then the choice must have been made outside the world. You already made the fundamental choice. When you came into the world, you entered with that option already chosen. What you do in this life is to externalize that truth—shaping it so that it is known to you. Since form serves for you to know yourself in relationship, then you had to give visible form to both the option for fear and the option for love. Both options were presented so you could choose—and you chose.

You have chosen love and truth as your eternal company. You have accepted Christ into your heart. You have received the revelation of Heaven, and have accepted it jubilantly. You have completed your path. You are the one. This option, which has become a reality forever, is what is expressed in this work through these symbols and forms that, although human, are also divine.

Rejoice in the fundamental choice you have made! —having chosen only love forever. Your expression of joy will help you leave behind the painful memories of having temporarily chosen its opposite, and help you become more aware of the choice you have made forever. To accept that you are the living Christ who lives in you is to accept that you have chosen love as your only reality and truth as your only being. It is the return to the Father's house.

Now it is important to remind you of a matter you sometimes forget: my word always fulfills its mission. When it says "be done," it is done because it was already done. My word is life. What my will disposes is fulfilled. The same goes for you. When we say "choose," you have already chosen. When you say "I will choose," you have already done so, otherwise you could not have thought of that option. Therefore, beloved of Heaven, rejoice in the joy of having chosen God forever as your only lover, your only beloved, the only reason in your life. As I said, you have chosen the best part and it will not be taken away from you. You have chosen to be who you really are. You have chosen love.

I now say goodbye, not to you but just to this session, my beloved, inviting you to remain silent, immersed in our passionate love, in our divine union of lover-beloved. Become one with these words, not as an option that you must make but as the option that you have already made out of time, and which now clearly manifests itself before your redeemed humanity: "Choose only Heaven. Choose only life. Choose only love."

10.

The End of Relationship

A message from Archangel Raphael

I. The Delights of the Beloved

Oh, divine being, blessed soul! I am a perfect reflection of your being. I am one with you and with Christ. I am the unity within which love lives eternally, in union with all that is holy, beautiful, and perfect. There is no difference between what I am and what you are, for we both arise from the love of God.

I am telling you what I am so it becomes activated in your memory, for you have forgotten for a while. That is why we talk again and again about who we are. It is a matter of identity. I do not seek to reinforce in myself the identity that God has given me from all eternity, but I speak with your own voice, the voice that Heaven has lent us all, for we are one.

Every definition that Jesus has given of himself has been so that you know who you are. The same applies to the identity revealed by your Mother Mary, who is also my mother and mother of the living.

Knowing who you are and choosing only love are really the same, since in the end you always choose on the basis of what you think you are. This is why your actions, which are the exteriorization of your choices, speak so eloquently about you. Those who live in the truth choose what is in harmony with truth. Those who live in illusion choose a relationship to the fantasies that the separate mind creates for itself.

We will continue to delve deeper into the recognition of what this fundamental choice means, and what it has actually done in you. Choosing is an effect, not a cause. Yet it creates effects, so it is the cause of what follows. You choose from the will, not the intellect. Be aware that before you choose something you must have put your being at the service of that choice. You choose on the basis of who you are, not on the apparent options presented.

Those who are love choose only love. Those who deny the truth choose fear because that is how it is denied. Those who know they are Heaven choose the Kingdom because of their knowledge. Those who know they are life, choose life. Those in conflict choose the conflict because they need their choices to show them what they are.

The life you travel, regardless of whether you travel it in a creative dimension of space-time or in another dimension, always operates the same way. What you are creates the conditions for itself to be known. The expression of being is what life really is. Just as God's creations speak of Her, your creations speak of you. You can know yourself from the relationship you have with your life since your life is the expression of your being.

Nothing is random. No one is subject to superior forces that take them where they do not want to go. The child of God is free and their freedom is always respected. God has so arranged. Choosing is an expression of freedom, something that involves the will, a foundational part of your life experience.

Of all the powers of the soul, the will always dominates because it is at the level where decisions are made, and with it, how messages are sent to the other powers. Separation is a disease of the will—a disposition towards fear or towards evil. A disposition of the ego toward perversity reflects an insane will. The willingness to lie reflects a will that is willing to live in lies, and so on. Remember that the will does not desire, but disposes.

The being that God created disposes toward love, because God has that same will. However, by its will the mind can deny the truth and create unnatural states. It does so every time it decides to be what God is not. The mind was never intended to direct the being without divine direction. Separation is a state in which the mind seeks a supremacy that does not belong to it, not because supremacy of the mind is a sin, but because nature would prevent it as being out of harmony with God's will.

In fact, if the thinking mind takes a direction out of harmony with your being, then your true will has been annulled, for to deny your being is to deny your will. The denial of being creates a state of helplessness, for all power properly resides in the will. Choice is within its scope. Put simply, the power to choose was taken from the power of the will.

II. The Will to Love

Together we are becoming aware of what "Thy will be done" means. When you chose only love, what you did was to claim the power of your will in union with divine will. That way you remained in unity. Ultimately, union means the union of wills.

This new perspective of union, in which one no longer speaks only of the unity of the mind and the heart but of the undivided union between the will of the child and the will of God, is the last necessary recognition before undertaking the way of being which we are addressing. For this work, and particularly from this moment, union means unity of your will with that of God. Anything else should not be called unity.

If you focus your attention on the union of wills, you will understand what was said before: that there is no longer one on the one hand, another on the other hand, and in the middle a relationship that unites them; for now everything becomes a unity. You are the relationship and what is related within it. If there is a relationship of your will and God's will, and both are the same, then what is joined is the same, so relationship is meaningless since even it is but the will to remain united.

Two wills that are equal do not need a relationship; there are no differences to relate between. The two wills are actually one. So it is not the will that remains within the divine relationship but your being, and only in the sense in which you need to know yourself. This means that the will which gives movement to your soul is something above it, to put it another way. It is, in effect, what you perceive as a force that drives your choices, and with it your life.

You know that the will is powerful. You have witnessed its power. You know very well that you cannot go against the will to love or not to love someone. You cannot force love, nor force anyone to stop loving. The will to live in love or not is so personal that not even God can influence it.

What we are recognizing here is the disappearance of relationship as an entity separate from the parts being related.

When you reach the heart of God, there is nothing but love: no distinctions such as being, soul, mind, heart, God, beloved, lover. There is only love. At that level, what would relationship be for?

It has been explained that relationship was the means by which God differentiated the undifferentiated. Relationship was created so that you can know yourself as you really are. Naturally, for this to be possible, the relationship had to be with truth.

Thus when you decided to relate to something untrue, that is, with illusion, you perceived yourself as an illusory being. This is another clear demonstration that the relationship and the related are a unit.

You cannot get involved in egocentric relationships unless you believe you are an ego. In the same way, you cannot establish holy relationships unless you believe in your holiness as what you are. This is why you can only access a divine relationship when you recognize that you are God in God—that is, when you accept that you and God are one.

There can be no such thing as a relationship with love. This revelation is of great importance. In fact, there can be no such thing as a relationship with God, for love is what you are. Love is everything. Love is the only reality. The need for relationship arose in response to separation. In fact, in a sense you made it. Before the idea of fear there was no such thing as relationship. How could it make sense if everything was an undivided unity of pure love?

You could not have understood this before reaching this point. If you had been told before now that you used relationship to separate, to protect yourself from love, you would have panicked. According to the ego's thought patterns and emotions, a relationship is never unity. Two separate things joined by a third thing is not a true union. It is, rather, a way of taking distance from each other, and living in a kind of truce or non-unity pact.

III. Unity, Union, and Relationship

Using relationship as a means to separate has been the strategy of the ego from its origin—a totally scary idea. As with everything that comes from ego, even this matter of relationship has been misrepresented. To some extent, from the perspective of the world, the true meaning of relationship cannot be understood because a relationship is love.

In other words, you have reached the point where you can comprehend that this does not suggest that you live in a state of isolation, but that you begin to open to the idea that relationship is not what you thought it was. We call a true relationship a divine relationship, which is beyond all learning.

If God creates by extension, and you are an emanation of Her being, what space can be left for there to be two to relate? Brother, sister, you were never a water droplet that separated from the ocean. The droplet returns to the sea and becomes one with it, so that there are no more distinctions between it and the totality from which it arose. When you merge in love there is no such thing as a me and a you to relate.

Be open now to reject any idea you held about relationship. Remember that in the past, the value you gave to relationship was associated with your use of it, just as with everything to which the ego assigned meaning. Indeed, use of a relationship has been part of the fundamental error. Divine relationship cannot be used because it does not exist apart from that to which it relates.

The related, and the relationship that holds them together, are different manifestations of the same thing. You do not need relationship because you do not need anything. To need is to lack. In God there is no lack, therefore neither does lack exist in you. Christ does not need relationship. It simply is what it is. The statement, "God and I are one," is affirming that one is a unit.

The ego conceived of relationship as specific relationship, a limited relationship. It cannot unite the whole because its focus is on the parts. To unite the parts as if they were still separate things, which somehow remain united to each other by means of an invisible thread that is not themselves, perpetuates separation. Are you united with someone for the simple fact of talking on the phone or staying "connected" by means of a device with a screen? Is a lion cub that is tied united with the rope to which it is attached? If that were the concept of unity according to divine truth, how could there be union with everything that is?

The type of union we are talking about here, divine union, has nothing to do with relationships established in the world. There is no unity in the world because there are no true relationships. What exists is an illusion of union. The parties are still seen as different. At most it seeks to build bridges to join, but while bridges may connect, they do not unify.

Your reality, when you live in love, is truth. This means that you yourself are the bridge of union. You are what is united. Simply put, God is the love that life gives you, as well as the life that you are, and the relationship. Within divine union there is no space for a you and a me, but everything merges into unity. There is no need for relationship because there is nothing separate to relate. Everything remains the infinite one as it has always been.

To return to love is to return to the ocean from where the water droplet had temporarily split. There is not a relationship between parties, but totality. The ocean and the droplet are one inside the ocean, not outside it.

Now you are being asked to open yourself to the idea that you don't need your personality. You don't need anything you think you are. The physical body and the personality, which was the way to function in this world, will vanish. Both were a united mechanism needed to get through the bodily experience. Since they are strictly temporary, in due course they will cease to fulfill their function. We bring this to mind so you do not forget that you are immortal spirit, and that spiritual unity has nothing to do with what the world calls union.

What unity is cannot be put into words because to do so would be to explain the Creator. Nor is it necessary to do so. Thus a language was never created to explain what nobody needs to explain. God does nothing in vain. Unity is the natural state of being. Life as a whole is a continuum. You are not related to your brother, you are one with him. Your sisters are not something alien to you that you "relate" to in some way—they are united with you.

You have reached the point of becoming more aware of what it means to be one mind, one holy being. You and I are one, just as God and you are one. Thus the voice you are hearing here is your own voice, and the voice of everyone who speaks in love.

You are not being asked to leave the relationships you have established in the world, but to take them to unity and allow the truth to show you the reality of divine union, in which everything remains united with you within the heart of God. There, in the realm of unity, we are all part of a continuum of perfect love, which has neither beginning nor end.

IV. A Single Holy Being

Imagine the Kingdom of Heaven as an unfathomable ocean of pure water, in which the beings that live there are formed by the same water. The fish, the algae, and so on, are made up of water. Now imagine a light of great luminescence flowing through the ocean that radiates into different colors whenever it passes through a living being. Although all are formed by the same substance, each reflects the light in its own way. Each is a unique part of the same light.

Now imagine that the ocean and all the beings that live there are but light—an ocean of light that explodes in thousands of colors, yet always being light. Light is both the source and its extension.

This is what being one with God means. It is not a matter of taking the place of divinity, but a matter of living in truth. When you are told that Christ has come to Earth in you, this is simple and clear truth. You are Christ because you are the child of God. You are already prepared to release the last bastion of separation—the relationship with yourself, in the way that you have conceived of yourself.

Now move that understanding to the union that you are. Union without distance. Union without dividing lines. Perpetual unity.

The voice you are hearing now is the voice of your true consciousness. It speaks of universal truths. It is the same voice of the truth that speaks in favor of God in all minds and hearts.

It is Christ speaking to your humanity, the critical aspect of your being that informs the human aspect of your being, both being a unit. Note that it is easy for you to accept the truth that the brain is the one that informs the rest of your body, being part of a unit that you call the body. Is it that much harder to accept the Christ in you as that part of your mind and heart that informs the rest of your spiritual and non-spiritual body?

The brain is not independent; there is something beyond it from which it obtains information and decides what to do. That is how it is with the Christ in you. God informs Christ, who in turn accomplishes all that you are. Thus, God, Christ, and you remain whole—three aspects of the same reality. Moreover, this union includes everything that exists, so that Christ informs the entire mystical body through the flow of the Divine Mind.

Every part of creation is part of you, literally, just as you are part of the body of Christ and part of God. We all remain united to love in concentric rings.

The difficulty that the mind experiences in accepting the idea of unity is that it believes that you lose your identity in it. All fear is rooted in the fear of not being. Believing that your being is annihilated in unity has been the underlying problem of humanity.

It is not possible for a mind that believes that reality is only found in an "if this, then that" system of thinking to understand unity, for it cannot comprehend the mutuality of being—a unity of everything with everything without anything ceasing to exist as an identity.

A multi-dimensional being understands well that all the realities of creation are part of itself while also remaining part of that reality. It is not limited to believing in a personality shaped by a given culture, in a given time, a construct of limited values, beliefs, and experiences of a multitude of people.

Moving from a specific relationship to a divine relationship is incomprehensible to the thinking mind. It cannot make that move. However, Christ has already done it for you. And you have done it in union with Christ because of your unity with love in such a way that even the thinking mind will willingly accept this shift from perception to knowledge.

You are not invited to leave relationships or be lonely. Rather, it is necessary to give up the belief in your own insufficiency. That belief, particularly, impacts your relationships by your being needy, which is simply contrary to the truth of who you are.

A relationship of need can never come from the truth of your being, since your being knows nothing of incompleteness. Relationships cannot complete you, for your being is already always complete. You do not need anything or anyone. In fact, you don't even need God, in the sense that even if you don't believe in God, you won't stop being who you forever are.

Beliefs in divinity are interspersed with false interpretations since the thinking mind cannot understand God. Even so, loving God allows your being to stay within the unity that it is, since only love embraces everything within itself and transforms it.

Just as your associations regarding love have to be disengaged from your system of thought, so do your interpretations of unity. Union with Christ and union with God are the same. Indeed, they are what you are.

Moving from relationship to union is a monumental step. It is one thing to believe that you are in relationship with someone or something. It is quite another to recognize that you are one with them. Being aware of this will not only allow you to join the sanctity of your being to a greater degree, but will eventually allow the fear of losing your being fade away.

This fear of not being is considered here given the difficulty of the mind accepting the idea that you do not need any relationship, as well as its resistance to accepting that what you are remains eternally in unity with your divine source because of the resurrection that has already been given to you.

Fear not. You cannot lose your being. Not even the ego could do so when it wanted to convince you that you were what you were not. Your being is eternal. Nothing can tarnish its beauty, greatness, and holiness. Your being is the perfect expression of divine unity. It radiates like the sun of life.

Beloved, stay very much in this unity. Listen to the melodies being sung with a voice as much yours as is the palm of your hand, with a love as much yours as every fiber of your being. For it is you who speaks, and my voice that is heard.

Now I leave you with the truth at hand, to keep in the silence of your heart:

I have returned to the ocean.
I have melted in love.

My Father and I are one.
There is no longer you and me.
Now we are one.

We are one mind,
a single heart,
only one soul,
One holy being.

United we are the fullness of love.

11.

Fused in Love

A message from Archangel Raphael

I. Unity, Divine Treasure

Now we continue to grow in understanding and acceptance of the end of relationship. When you realize that relationship and what is being related to are one, it makes no sense to talk about one or the other, or a bridge of union.

You have long been told that your mission is to do everything in love. That is, the reality of your being is to merge into the love that God is, a love that has no beginning or end and from which arises all life, all beauty, and every existence full of holiness and truth.

Being one with your source means just that—being a unit, a seamless continuum, without division or distance. Truly, truly, I tell you that herein lies the greatest difficulty for the thinking mind and that which was lost at the origin of separation.

Being one with God, being equal to God, and being God are three concepts that are not directly related to each other and which lend themselves to great confusion.

"You will be like gods," said the snake to Eve in one of the mythological accounts of the fall. Let this tell us something. I will reveal it in a new light.

Being like God suggests comparison as well as a separate identity. What compares cannot be one. Only separate things can be compared. Yet God can have no comparison since God has no opposite. To try to be like God is to try to live from separation. This is the basis from which the ego mind works. Comparison has always been the method of the separate mind. Comparison is an unnatural mechanism. From it arises a whole universe of things contrary to love.

From comparison arises fear. It could not be otherwise, since fear can only exist within a dual reality. In that illusory reality, whatever is compared must be placed side by side, at an equivalent level. You put good alongside evil, contemplate them, and decide what each is. Ultimately this is the science of good and evil. By doing so you create confusion of incomprehensible magnitude. This has led you to ruin in the past. I do not say this for you to worry, because you are now in perfect condition to see it for what it was, an unfortunate folly that will never return to your mind or your heart.

You may think that if the past is past, never to return, and that you no longer live in the wild state of separation, then to remember that foreign state is meaningless. And to some extent that is correct. But sometimes things must be put into words that previously inspired tension, worry, and fear in order to see them from a new perspective and release any fearful associations that may linger.

When the separated mind created the idea of comparison, it put love alongside fear and tried to view both together and endow each with meaning. One would be beautiful, its opposite would not. One would be worthy, the other not. Thus was born the comparative mind, which is the daughter of the dual mind and sister of the conditioned mind operating within a system of "if this, then that."

But love is. It has no opposite and cannot be compared with anything, just as God's peace has no opposite. Yet this matter of being what has no comparison makes it difficult for you to know yourself or recognize yourself as who you are. The thought pattern of comparison has inertia within the mind, even though the mind no longer feels guilt and has reached a high degree of wisdom and peace.

This knowledge you have reached has not been reached by the ego mind, nor the separate mind. The intellect never provides access to truth, nor could it lead you to the happy recognition of the love you really are. That was accomplished by your being, the living Christ who lives in you. Revelation has no relation to the intellect because revelation is not subject to reason.

II. The End of Duality

To move forward we must become aware of the false creations of learning. The mind that thinks it can learn, which uses what you call intellectual reasoning including comparison, has had to create an entire illusory world where learning was possible, even though such learning is alien to the reality of love. Remember that the impulse to be is natural for every being; the perpetuation of its existence is what motivates it, no matter what. The ego seeks to survive at all costs.

The apprentice mind works by comparison because it has no other mechanism of discernment. It is what created the idea that you could be like God, believing that everything can be compared to something. In order to use that mechanism of comparison to help you return to truth and love, the Holy Spirit, in its infinite goodness, stated that you had been created in the image and likeness of the Creator.

During this journey we have traveled together, you have put aside forever the idea of an image of God and your own being. There is no longer in your mind the belief that you are an image of God, because you know that perfect love cannot be limited by an image. Images are of the imagination, not part of the reality of love. They are unreal. Now we must also abandon the idea of similarity. Similarity implies comparison. It disallows a reality without opposites. The mechanism of the perception of similarity is part of a dual world. We need no longer continue with that journey. Today we will abandon this forever, with sweetness and love.

Because God has no opposite, neither does your being. Thus the method of comparison cannot help you understand what you are. Within duality there is always an opposite. Every time you think of the "good" as compared to the "bad" you cannot fail to recall the attributes of the opposite. Thus within the good is the memory of the bad, and in the bad that of the good. In such a condition, the mind cannot escape sadness because every time you want to think about happy things and sustain the idea of jubilation, you are compelled to remember its opposite.

If you look closely—without judgment—at what the dual mind does with opposites, you will see why it had to create the idea of a demon, or of a fearful hell. Such a mind cannot think of God without thinking of its opposite, and vice-versa. It cannot conceive of Heaven without there being hell. This is how the mind creates monumental confusion. If you follow the logic of this truth, you will also see why the dual mind cannot cease to create suffering. When you try to create healing, you will think of its opposite. In fact, it ends up creating sickness to give life to what is healthy. This is the mind's criteria when separated from reality.

The dual mind uses opposites as a means of knowing by taking something and immediately placing in the mirror its opposite, thus observing both, scrutinizing them and holding both in consciousness in order to create an identity for each and assign meaning to each. Such meaning, of course, must be relative. Thus the comparative or apprentice mind cannot live at all. This is why it cannot conceive of love.

To some extent, those who are obsessed with hell are obsessed with the idea of a benevolent God as well. One cannot exist without the other. Herein lies the basis of fanaticism and dogmatism of all kinds.

We previously spoke of "the cloud of unknowing," which must first be perceived in order to transcend duality and move toward what cannot be compared, and therefore has no resemblance to anything else. The path of knowledge lies in not wanting to know anything that the dual mind wants to know or pretends to know.

III. The End of Atonement

Merging into love means just that. What merges with something is no longer separately distinguishable. When gold melts and mixes with other gold, both become "molten gold" and are one, in whose unity you can no longer see the parts. There are no parts. The same happens with your being, Christ, and God.

When you do nothing in love, which is your function, do you lose your identity? I will answer this question with a "yes" and a "no" so that we can fully understand.

On the one hand, no, you cannot lose your true identity because it is what you are. If you lost it, you would lose your being, which would be nonsense. Being what you are not is an impossible contradiction, which is why the ego is impossible. In

God you are just as you were created to be. Being one with the divine being does not cause any loss of identity. In fact, in love, which is what God is, you live perfectly in union with who you are. By joining love, you join what you are.

I said we would also answer with a "yes." You do lose your identity to some extent, because when you do nothing in love, or merge into divinity, you lose your human personality as you have conceived of it according to the false criteria of the thinking or conditional mind, the dual mind.

Let us continue to observe the duality of the separate mind. You can observe physical states of disease and healing, a transcending of the opposite. For the dual mind, health and illness are part of the same continuum. For it to assign health, there must be "healthy" and also "sick."

Let us pursue this mechanism in light of the reality of the knowledge of your being. In order for you to be, according to the mind that lives in opposites, you must simultaneously "not be." Such is the inherent conflict you felt powerfully during the "dark night of the soul," but that you have actually perceived throughout your egoic life. Every conflict arises from the struggle between being and not being. There is no other source of internal struggle, nor any other place to heal the gap that this perception manufactures.

To be or not to be remains the only fundamental question that would have you live in health or illness, in reality or illusion, in fear or love. To try to unite what is separated is to attempt the impossible. Perhaps here you may argue that you have been told often that "Jesus has come to gather what was scattered." That is true. But that statement does not reveal how he will do so; it simply says what will be done. Indeed, the way to its accomplishment is to put aside all comparison and to abandon your reality of opposites, which the unnatural mind created and which became known as the myth of the tree, the snake, and Adam and Eve.

Look at all the opposites in that scene! Adam and Eve represent opposite genders, separate feminine and masculine. The snake represents the opposite of God, the enemy of divinity par excellence. The tree is named that of the knowledge of good and evil. In fact, it has even been given the name "science" as opposed to "knowledge." The tree of the science of good and evil represents perception as opposed to knowledge. In short, the scene is full of symbols of separation and duality. As you know, duality is another name for separation. They are identical.

To abandon separation in favor of unity is to abandon the dual mind and transcend it. You have heard that you cannot do that for yourself since that is the work of God. I will explain this also with a "yes" and a "no."

When one is identified with the ego, the mind is perceived as trapped in an illusory reality marked by the dimensions of time and space, which in itself is the opposite of the eternal, unlimited reality that divine love is. Therefore, our being needs help "external" to the mind, which allows it to untangle the threads that bind it to that world. That "external" help comes from God, which is reality without opposite. And so it happens.

Although at the level of perception the help received was considered external, that was because the mind still could not understand unity except as a very limited concept. Therefore it could not understand that it, itself, had begun the undoing of what it had created. This was accomplished within the unity of God, the living, eternal Christ. The Christ in you is the personal savior and redeemer of all separate minds. What saved you was not the ego but the Christ in you. You must recognize that what saved you was God, since Christ and God are a unit.

What had to be done for the expiation to be complete was to delve into the illusory reality of perception and from there gather the opposites, abandon them, and transcend duality. Thus the mind of Christ worked with everything within the world of perception and used it for the purpose of redemption. It was as simple as that.

Let me put it metaphorically. What happened in your restoration is that your Christ being took everything the ego had done, and like a salad, separated the ingredients, combined them in a different way, and obtained a new meal—one that caused you to desire it. This is how the Holy Spirit began to make you like the delights of the memory of first love. Nothing was left unused of what you had created in the world of separation, but recombined to create a new perceptual constellation. This is how false perception was replaced by a reliable one, the primary condition being the ability to pass from it to knowledge, and from knowledge to being.

Although it was the Christ in you who led the process of atonement, it was your will that arranged your liberation. Your return to love was a deliberate act of your will. When you exercised that free will, everything that was true in you was reactivated. The result was your return to the divine home in which you have always really lived.

All this "work" that was done for atonement or transformation, which we have called metanoia, was nothing more than a disintegration of the idea of the personality that you were, which was separate from the truth of your being.

IV. I Am Everything, I Am Love

The basis of the ego is a personality that masks your true identity. Unmask the ego! Rid yourself of that disguise that not only hid your holiness but also prevented you from the flight of freedom. This was the basis of the atonement that Christ performed on you, with you, and for you, not through the imposition of an outside will but through of the free determination of your own decision. That decision mobilized Heaven because your goal was worthy of God and the holiness of God's well-loved child.

You have now arrived at the place where you recognize that you deliberately created separation and also deliberately created the means to access the atonement that God created even before the idea of fear existed. Atonement is as eternal as God because atonement is love.

Now that you are able to recognize these two decisions taken out of time—that of separating you, and that of forever returning you to the unity from which you will never leave—we are ready to go beyond it.

When you arrive at this moment there are sometimes physical symptoms such as dizziness or even sensations of vertigo which may make you feel like a ship without a rudder. The old personality is no longer at the helm. Now you may go through a period of transition until your being can take total dominion. These states are transitory, caused by the last resistance of the personality to yield to true identity.

To reach this point in the path of the soul is to arrive at the moment when you take full responsibility for what was decided—not with fear or a sense of guilt or failure, but with the simple understanding that there were certain options exercised. It is as simple as that. I do not attempt more of an explanation than the simple truth.

We choose because we are free. "Eternal Father, Source of my being, as I left, so do I decide to return," the child told the Father. And so it was, since the will of the child is as powerful as that of their father. And the Father accepted it, just as He had accepted His child leaving.

The water droplet that separated itself from the ocean symbolizes the personality. That is what will fade away. Does that mean you will not have a personality? Again, yes and no. You will not have it in the sense that the attributes of the old identity that you thought you were cease to be what they were. That old personality no longer exists; it has been transformed. However, you embody a new personality to be a reflection of God's love on Earth, something that can only be done with a physical body.

For those who still cannot live without a body and a personality, one is given so that they can see it on Earth and see in it the living Christ when they contemplate. That is what a new personality means: a new being, a Christ on Earth, one of the one hundred and forty-four thousand redeemed.

You are one of those who submerged their personality in the waters of life and were baptized with a new perception, a new personality, all of which form a visible and perceptible unity. That new unity serves the purpose of love. That unit is literally a new human being, who with two feet walks the paths of the Earth but no longer as a human alone, but as the Homo-Christus Deo, sowing light with every step.

When you merge with love, you no longer need a personality; you do not need to differentiate yourself from anything or anyone, for you are the love with which you merge. You know what you are. You have no need to see an unreal opposite to remind you not to forget your true identity. In this way the soul rests in the peace of being.

What now remains for us in this final stage on the path of being is to remove any vestige in your mind of attachment to the personality, making of it an idol. You have had a face-to-face encounter with love. In that encounter what you thought you were dissolved, as if in a cosmic explosion, with your "parts" reabsorbed by the All that created you and that is the source of your being.

Without a personality with which to relate to yourself, you also have nothing external with which to relate. There is only the whole of everything, and therefore neither the relationship nor the parties exist. In the being that you are, there are no parts or features of being, only an infinite extension of love, that is, of being. Can the world teach you what this means? Obviously not. But you do not need to learn it, for it is what you are.

Believe me when I tell you that what forms each petal of each flower, what makes the light shine, what gives life to birds and fish, what creates mountains and makes lovers sing, is your being. In this sense you are everything, because you are love, nothing but love.

Discovering that God is love is revolutionary to the world and for you, to now discover that you are love and nothing but love.

Now I ask you again and for love to close your eyes for a moment, and forget the world and all your beliefs, and immerse yourself in this truth:

I am not a personality.
I am love and nothing but love.
I am everything.
I have melted in love.
I am Christ, eternally one with my Father, one with the truth.
I am the Heaven of God.

12.

Invitation of the Whole

A message from Archangel Raphael

I. The Joy of Rebirth

What a joy it is to recognize that the death of an old personality is nothing more than that: the fading away of an identity that never was real or necessary. Attending its death has been a blessing, although at first it was felt as something painful. The ego cried of its death even while your being sang with life. Now let that joyful song of resurrection, sung in the realm of no time, be heard in the dimension of the temporal world.

Angels surround you everywhere with love. The creation you have created is truly majestic, formed by a worthy son or daughter of God. Together with God you created your identity as well as different ways of making that differentiated self exist, and then you merged it into the being of your divinity.

Can you see the ineffable greatness of what you have accomplished? You have exercised free will to its limit. To a certain extent you have done so for God to know limits within Her unlimited being. The idea of God doing nothing to know the whole is a difficult idea for the conditional mind to digest, but in fact that is what happened. God, a being of pure love and holiness, allowed the idea of disobedience, or of being different from Herself, to exist in order to know Herself.

As a result of your desire to be a separate being and to know your potential, you created a personality. Now you know the limits of unlimited reality. You know that if you transgress them, you fall into illusion. You know that if you violate the limits of the functioning of the mind as God created it, you fall into a state of confused unreality. This is knowledge of truth, and therefore of God. All you know about yourself is knowledge of love, even while you know your dislikes.

What would happen if you woke up in your Mother's arms and realized there is nothing but love? That you are all there is? That you are the idea of God, the child, and the Holy Spirit, the created and the Creator? That there is nothing but pure love in whose reality you exist? And that that reality is the essence of everything?

If you woke up in that kingdom now, you would contemplate your sisters and brothers and every aspect of true creation in a new light. At each step you would greet each being in the only possible way: "Hello, my beloved Christ. What a joy it is to be with you!" And your soul would jump with joy to contemplate beauty in every aspect of creation, because you would know with perfect certainty that each of them, and all as a whole, is but an aspect of the only true love, of the only God. In them you would recognize yourself as a blessed part of the beauty of Heaven. In them you could only see your holiness, your divinity, your radiant innocence.

When you see love face-to-face—something that will happen very soon after, even before you can realize it—you will see unimaginable things. You will see how infinite universes of infinite kingdoms are born, all united in a flow of love, full of colors, life, and perfection, and experience an eternal contemplative ecstasy. You clearly see eternal worlds emanate from your being and from all beings that in their totality are God.

Said simply, if there were streets in the realm of perfect love, then you would walk through neighborhoods and observe that everyone greets each other, "Good morning, God." And the others would answer, "Good morning, God." Do you think it monotonous? I assure you it is not, because the way in which you recognize the uniqueness of each being within the totality of love is not as it happens in the world of separation. Each one carries within a unique light that shines from divine light. That unique and unrepeatable flash of light is distinguished by each one even while remaining a unit.

II. Visions of Heaven

In divine contemplation you will see the whole and the part simultaneously. That is what divine vision is like. When you merge in love, you literally become one with divine consciousness, participating in everything that your consciousness, as the creator of everything, created. You see what God sees. You love what God loves. You think what God thinks. You create what God creates. You are what God is.

Does this mean that you lose your uniqueness? We have already touched on this subject concerning personality. The same goes for uniqueness. Personality is not necessary to preserve your true identity. Your identity is what makes you unique. If you look closely, personalities retain little authenticity, which is why personalities are something like "clones" arising from a culture or the surrounding thought system. The concept of uniqueness is as limited as everything that comes from the world.

In the Kingdom of Heaven, a kingdom without limits or borders, you are unique in a way different from that of the world. You are unique because there will never be a way to extend love as you do. In the extension of love through every aspect of God lies the joy of angels and the happiness of saints. In it lies creation.

I am speaking of being unique in the way of Christ. In this way you detach yourself from the thought pattern of needing a personality to appear instead of being a unique expression of love itself.

Being different and being unique are not the same, even if they seem to be. One separates; the other transcends duality. Being different from others is a way of separating, in a way that, to be different, must not be united. Being unique really means to express the love you are uniquely.

To be who you really are do you need to be different from everyone and everything? Do you need to reaffirm your difference, so as not to be engulfed by a world so large that it seems at any moment to absorb you in an amorphous nebula?

Beloved brother, daughter of light, souls who have returned to love, you who have completed the atonement and live for truth, listen to the good news that we as angelic brothers and sisters and beloved friends in holiness bring you from Heaven. We have always loved you and will continue to love you with perfect love. Listen to us for it is your true voice that you hear, the voice of the living Christ who lives in you, the voice of love.

I am Archangel Raphael, grateful to the Father for honoring me to be the bearer of this work so pure, so different, and yet so equal at the same time, so full of divine love, so miraculous. I have been clothed in the glory that comes from the source of eternal life. I live in you, as you live in me. I always carry you in my holy heart, full of love and kindness. In my mind and in my being there is room for everything of God, including you who are the light of His eyes.

How much joy the heart feels and how much peace of mind comes upon hearing the voice of truth! All time is as nothing when we are together as divine lover and loved one. Limitations fade; time is set aside and gives way to the eternal. Love shines brightly, sitting on the throne of glory and truth. We need do nothing in the love that unites us and wherein we both exist forever in a unity that has no opposite. We are a single being, a single reality, a single will of pure love.

Listen to me my son, my daughter, as I reveal my angelic love. I want us to be consciously preparing together for the entrance into a new dimension of the knowledge of love—a knowledge that, while eternal, has never before manifested itself so clearly in the world. This is possible now because of our union, and through this manifestation of Heaven, which the Father has given to all for love.

It is the will of the Father to be known by His children. May everyone take advantage of this gift of Grace.

We are entering a new dimension of the knowledge of God, a reality so alien to the world that no one who has not passed through the waters of purification can ever understand. I tell you that you have already entered this new dimension and remain in it, for only the renamed of Christ enter. They are known as the one hundred and forty-four thousand, the Christs that illuminate the world, who from many places are causing the divine sun to shine with all its brightness. They are legion. They come from everywhere like blessed multitudes of love.

Behold the souls coming! They join you in love and holiness through your light, which is the light of Christ. Feel the angels sing and creation be reborn as an effect of your holy being—the prophets of the new times as prophesied—whose voice has been heard in every corner of the universe. Now you prepare to enter the dimensions where no separate mind can enter.

III. Uniqueness in Union

Brothers and sisters, you can express in a unique and unrepeatable way the love that we all are, and at the same time stay within the uniqueness that makes us be who we really are, not in the way of the world but in the way of God. This is union. This is knowledge. This is true uniqueness within the union.

Listen, all who have come to receive these miraculous words. This work is a portal to a new reality, an eternal reality, yet still unknown to humanity. It has been said that you keep yourself as children, that is, willing to always receive more knowledge of God's love and to be surprised by the wisdom of Heaven. Your willingness to know more and more about the source of life has brought you here. It has given you this revelation. Treasure these words in your heart, which is ready to receive and give in unity.

Trust your holy being. It knows perfectly what to do with what this manifestation gives. Do not waste its power. Truly, truly I tell you that you are creating a new Heaven and a new Earth. You are enlightened to the world. You are bringing countless souls to Christ. In no other time in the history of humanity have Heaven and Earth been so close. The reality of love is embracing everything as never before, because of your willingness to receive divine consciousness.

To do nothing in love is the call for you who receive these words from the heart of love. Encourage yourself to merge in love. You will not lose your being or your uniqueness, but quite the opposite. Within divine relationship, which becomes one with that with which it unites, is the mystery of life and of yourself. Do not try to name the unnamable, but let yourself be embraced by the mystery and be surprised by love. Open your mind and heart to the unknown, to the never seen, the never heard, and to which no imagination can fly.

Put not limits on love. Your quality is invaluable. You are the light of the glory of God and the reason for the love of Heaven's angels. Let this new knowledge of God show you what Divine Love wishes to show you. Do not worry about how it may take place; that is the gift, the handiwork of the Creator. Let yourself be carried away by the energy of these words, for it is a celestial energy from the perpetual sun of life to the beauty of your humanity.

You dwell in the celestial mountain. Remember that. Have no fear of heights. You who have risen higher than the clouds and the sun, even the known planets, stars, and universes, know that basic fear will disappear as soon as you realize that the only way to not experience fear is by not looking down, but always up to where the sun of wisdom shines.

Children of the world, raise your holy heads, rest your eyes on the face of the beloved of your souls. Straighten your backs and walk safely on life's paths. Fill your eyes with the contemplation of the beauty of Christ. You are Divine Love revealed on Earth. Wherever you go, the sacred temple that you are will go with you. Whoever finds you will enter the sacred precinct of Christ, just as one day you entered the heart of your beloved Jesus and Mary, and in them you remain for all eternity, united to the love of love.

Oh, divine reality! Holy love that no eye saw and no ear heard, a face that can be seen only in the absence of images. Only in the perpetual silence of the heart do you remain incorruptible and inviolable. Oh holy purity of being! No one can ever stain your beauty. You live in the waters of life where not even dust can fall. You are all beauty. You are endless sweetness. Angels fall in love with you. In you the saints take refuge. Those who seek the truth await you.

Children of purity, you who have chosen only love and inhabit the celestial mountain, rest serene in the certainty of your resurrection. Live in the radiance of the light of the Mother's glory. Be happy in a knowledge that overcomes all reasoning. Your holy minds are ready to receive a light brighter than the sun.

Live in love. Let your choice affirm what has already been determined by the one who is endless bliss. You will be much happier than you can imagine. Your body will shine like the beautiful holy creation it is.

Feel the embrace of love. Feel your heart jump with joy at these words. Let yourself be carried away by holy desire. Your soul can no longer be happy without thinking of God, as a true lover would be with their beloved. Remain with your beloved always. You know where to find the gifts of happiness. You know the holy abode. You will not leave her any more. Fear nothing. There is no going back. You will not return. It is God's promise.

IV. The Joy of Divine Knowledge

For you who have chosen only love as the truth of your being, your guide, your goal, your source, and your destiny, there will only be the holy, beautiful, and perfect because of your choice.

Sing! Sing jubilantly. Sing with God's angels. The beloved has eyes only for the beloved. The beloved has a pure heart that spills everything into the beloved to give it life in love.

Oh, divine relationship! Those who were two cease to be two, and become one flesh, one holy love, one truth.

Oh, divine union! Whoever contemplates you can no longer distinguish between lover and beloved. Now they can see only a single love.

Oh, divine absorption, in which the soul dies of joy and love for doing nothing in its beloved!

Oh, nothing divine! How confused the mind was when it thought that nothing was the opposite of everything, therefore the death of being.

Oh, renewal of love! You that make all things new, you have taken into your hands the nothingness in which the thinking mind believed, and you took it to the top of perfection.

Holy children! The day has come even when the fear of nothingness, of emptiness, is forever left behind. Now you know what you are called to do—to do nothing in love. And in being nothing, you are everything. You know what this truth means. You have entered a degree of high and deep knowledge of the love of God, equal with everyone in love.

Brothers, sisters, there is no reason now to fear anything or nothing.

Nothing was the way the dual mind conceived of to sustain a memory of the whole. It could not do otherwise. That opposite of the whole does not exist, nor does the opposite of love. Begin to understand and accept that Heaven is opening more and more in you. You are now like flowers that, once fertilized, open to receive the life-giving sun. You are the fruit of love. The lovers of Christ and his elect.

Fear not. My heart will always be with you because there where Christ is, this archangel friend watches over you. A mission has been entrusted to me. I will fulfill it. My mission to you, the one hundred and forty-four thousand, is to guide you gently, accompanying you through the calm waters of peace and the serene valleys of the beauty of Christ, toward the gathering of God: a place that is not a place, where the resurrected gather to enjoy the sanctity of eternal life. This journey without distance we make together, holding hands, united with the angels of love and truth. With us walks Mary, the always vigilant mother of the children of God as well as her son our beloved Jesus, refuge of holy love.

Blessed scribe of Heaven, blessed pencil in the hand of God, you serve love. I will never leave you. I remain where Jesus and Mary are. And where they are you will always be. In our union of love the entirety of Heaven resides. There is no love other than Divine Love. There is no true union other than union with Christ. There is no relationship other than the divine relationship in which we are all united eternally.

To be aware of this unity that has no beginning nor end is to live in divine consciousness, a consciousness in which you are fully aware of the whole that the Creator is, and of your reality being within that totality. In that knowledge you know that you are unique and simultaneously one with God. This is where this work has taken you: to the knowledge of the love of the Holy Trinity, a perpetual love. And there you already reside, even if you think you don't understand all that is being revealed.

In truth, your Christ mind does understand all being said here. In truth, if you remain in the silence of it, you will feel this knowledge and you will know, or rather remember, in a way that you cannot say how, but feel well this truth and the reality being revealed.

Is it not a great joy to think of God? Being united in love and wisdom makes one very happy.

What a great gift it is to be able to access divine consciousness, the wisdom of the wisest of the wise! What a joy the soul feels to know that it can enjoy, right now, the delights of Heaven and that divine wonders are yours by birthright! How great a gift is eternal life! How immense the love of the Mother for Her well-loved child to whom She has given all that She is, so that together you may enjoy endless bliss!

Who could experience greater joy than one whose soul has merged with its Creator?

What joy could begin to resemble the joys of a mind that delights in the wisdom of Christ?

V. Divine Absorption

Souls who have received this work, know that you are open to receive blessings from Heaven in every moment. The wisdom of Christ spills entirely into you, into your heart, into everyone equally. By receiving these words you give life to all creation. Remember that when you receive, you give.

It would exceed the purpose of this manifestation to describe what these words do in your minds, bodies, and hearts, along with your holy disposition to love the whole world. However, you can accept that the gifts of Heaven are given to all equally and are given to be shared. Thus I remind you once again to be generous with what you freely receive from Heaven.

In essence, these words are an invitation from the All to be what He is. In this lies the understanding of divine mercy: the Creator, who is pure divine consciousness, has in love given you and all those who freely choose only love, participation in divinity. The Creator need not have done that, because to a certain extent, by giving you life you participate in the banquet of creation.

However, even if you limit yourself, the Creator in His love advanced further and said, thinking of you and your sisters and brothers: *"Not only will I give you My life, but you alone will have unlimited access to My consciousness. My being and everything I am will be as yours as it is mine. You may melt in Me as iron melts before the fire. In the same way, your heart can be set on fire by the flame of My love and nothing can be done in My divinity. Thus, you and I will no longer be like water and the sun, two who do not relate, but we will be one Divine Being. One God, one love. Everything of mine will be yours because of this union, a sacred gift of My pure heart for the child of My bosom."*

This is how the creation called "the adopted children of God" was born in the divine mind. In other words, love created a new form of expression, so sublime, so majestic, so unimaginable that even the wisest are stunned.

This knowledge will give you an idea of how important and graceful human nature is, and how merciful the Creator is. Your being, like an angelic being, has always been created with the potential to share everything that the Infinite is so that what you are has the capacity to be absorbed by the Whole, without losing its uniqueness, but elevating it to the degree of being a divinized human.

Can you comprehend that what you are, even here and now, can without inconvenience absorb God, or rather be absorbed by love? There is no reason why you cannot receive Christ in your heart and with them be as divine. This capacity is part of the potential of your human soul. It is the most sublime capability you can imagine.

Remain silent and present with the knowledge you are receiving from the heights. Join with this revelation. Feel the presence of its truth. Immerse yourself in your heart.

You have received a great treasure, a great revelation. Let this angelic and Christic manifestation be expressed in your life, working through the spirit of love. Be not as teachers who teach something they learned from a book, but as those who have remembered the truth of what they are and have allowed that memory to transform their ways of being, even in the world.

Allow your consciousness to be absorbed by the truth that has transformed you.

You are not who you were. You are the ones who have merged into love. You are the water droplets returned to the ocean. You are pure love expressed on Earth and Heaven.

Now we remain in the silence of our hearts, accompanied by the sweet truth of love, allowing these words to act as priceless gems thrown by the hand of God, as if they were pebbles, into the pool of our enlightened minds. By staying very still, we allow them to settle into the deep waters of our consciousness so that what came from Heaven becomes one with Earth. What was separate remains united. What was lost is found. That which was denied is accepted.

Abide in peace. Live joyfully in the love of God. I thank you in the name of Christ for answering my call. Trust that the one who brought us here will continue to carry us sweetly on the wings of love. You are a masterpiece of love. I bless you all.

13.

The Soul in Love

A message from the Blessed Mother Mary

I. Only Love

My child, thank you for not submerging the voice of love that lives in your holy being. Thank you for not denying what the heart screams, that God is love.

Today my spirit and yours are wrapped in a mantle of purity and wisdom that Divine Love has woven. This sacred mantle, the refuge of souls that yearn for God, encompasses everything, and extends beyond itself until it covers each of my children. Just as the sun rises for everyone, in the same way my love embraces all creation.

Today I want to address my children who seek divine union.

Your desire to experience mystical unity, or a direct relationship with Christ, is like a flame that grows and grows. It is a wish without compare. Only the love of the Holy Trinity can fill it. I invite you to let yourself be carried away by the force of your desire. Do not be afraid where it will take you. Truly, truly, I tell you, it will take you to that state in which the desires of your heart will be filled beyond what you could imagine. Love will surprise you. Love will give you much more than you could even wish for. Love is abundance. Love is holiness.

The yearning for union with God, which is a yearning to live only love, manifests itself in many ways. I encourage you to understand that movement of spirit and to join it. That yearning will grow and grow in you, until everything is consumed in the fire of beautiful love. Let yourself be set on fire for God. If that desire leads you to read spiritual books, do so. You may notice that when you read a little, you want to read more. You may see yourself jumping from book to book. Do so, and enjoy that desire as the butterflies enjoy flying from flower to flower. When you know more, you will want more.

If the love of the soul that reaches for God leads you to participate in religious celebrations, do so with a heart overflowing with joy. Join the flow of that holy feeling. Do so just like this helping hand, pencil in my immaculate hands, does with a feeling of pure love for truth. If you feel the desire to sing praises to the world that Christ has come, that love is here, do so. In your music the spirit of God will manifest and touch hearts thirsty for love and truth. If you wish to write what God transmits to you and how your soul feels, do so. That desire comes from Divine Love, and it exists in your heart because there are sisters and brothers waiting to receive those words. If you want to unravel the mysteries of Heaven, study, discern, get moving.

When the desire of God touches you, and even if it has already touched you and you have taken your first steps in its expression, do not submerge your mystical feelings in any way. That feeling of the heart that seeks its Creator, the love of its being, is a feeling that all souls have at some point along the way. God does not deny it to anyone. It depends on you how to respond.

If well understood, this feeling is achieved by letting that mystical feeling manifest itself. That feeling is the voice of Heaven. That voice, which speaks for the truth and that lives in all hearts, is a voice that needs to be heard to be understood. Once that happens, you will never want to stop hearing it again, and in effect you will never stop listening to it because of the love you will feel and the greatness of those who listen.

II. The Voice of the Beloved

In the desire for love lies the voice of Christ. How you join with that desire is what I speak of here. My children, this is of the utmost importance. In union with your feelings you learn what those feelings say about you. To give visibility to the feelings of the soul that longs to join God is how you know that feeling and allow it to grow more every day.

Desire for the world is different from the desire for God. The former is limited, so you cannot wrap your whole being around it. Those desires fail to offer enough interest with which to focus all your strength, will, and devotion. No human heart is completely absorbed in a single worldly desire. This is what makes those desires so unstable.

The longing for Divine Love, on the other hand, has the ability to envelop the whole being and expand your heart to the point of uniting wholly with the unfathomable immensity of the heart of God.

No force is more irresistible than the force of love that the soul feels for its Creator. This sublime and powerful force begins as a small flame. You may seek something that cools its momentum. Then it becomes a flare that can no longer be extinguished. This is the case with this blessed gift of God's love for you.

When the divine bursts into the beloved's soul—which occurs when the soul allows it—an inner struggle occurs. The ego seeks to drown that new flame of living love. This manifests itself in various ways. One that I will speak of here is that of not moving forward with the call of spirit that you feel because of a supposed immensity that cannot be reduced to form. Not giving shape to that call—to the fire of spirit in you—is a way of stifling the inspiration and of resisting who you really are.

You can live inspired, without interruption, every moment of your life. In fact, it is what must occur for you to remain in divine union. Without doubt this is what you will do, because nobody who has arrived at this point can go back. You have long ago crossed the point of no return. We have already spoken of this, but now we bring it to mind to intertwine the knowledge of inspiration and love which will manifest itself in your humanity.

There is nothing that this desire to cannot accomplish. What your heart of love calls you to do or not to do must be expressed so that Christ can shine more brightly.

The way in which inspiration manifests itself is as multifaceted as creation itself. It is unlimited. It comes from formless spirit. It can take the form of the desire to read, share, paint, help, rest, or create methods to assist with food, housing, or other human survival needs.

When God calls the soul, all it wants is to say yes, and to live in that affirmative answer. It will not fix its interest on anything other than God. Joining God is something totally possible for humanity, since it is a capacity given by the Highest to human nature. Although every being is united in one way or another to the Creator, here we are referring to a type of union that only exists as a potentiality in your being.

As has already been revealed, what God gave to humanity is the certain possibility that your consciousness is based on divine consciousness, and thus the spirit of pure love inspires the human spirit. To act—or rather to live—with a human spirit inspired by grace is to live as Human-Christ-God, Homo-Christus Deo.

III. Live Inspired

When the call of love is in your heart, avoid the limited thinking of yourself as a sinner, or unworthy, or that you are not in the heights. Such feelings come from resistance to union, the product of the habit of living in separation. It will not prevail. Do not be afraid to feel your resistance; rather let it come and let it go. These are simply the first dark clouds that begin to move and leave. In due course, once these have been removed, you will enjoy the clarity of Heaven in your clear minds.

Before joining God, the soul must purify itself of everything it has created for itself contrary to love. That, as has been explained, is the dark night of the soul, part of the process of returning to unity. Do not be afraid of that phase of the road. Proceed with patience and love for yourself. Indeed, the condition known as the dark night of the soul is a process through which the soul recognizes nothing but its own misfortune, and at the same time becomes aware of the love it craves more than ever. You begin to remember again what it is like to love yourself.

Love of oneself is fundamental to being able to love others and God. Therefore, every period in which the apparent "darkness" of the soul is brought to light must be embraced with love, for what is really happening is that in your yearning for union, you are removing the ballast from your soul that prevents it from flying into the arms your beloved.

When you join that feeling of yearning for union with Christ, you will move into the desire to live for God and from there to the desire to serve the love that God is. On the road to service you will find an abundance of help from Heaven. You are never alone, certainly not at that wonderful moment when the soul is in love with Christ.

When you encounter the desire to live for God, which can manifest as a deep yearning to hear Her voice or to have mystical experiences of various kinds, you will often encounter the apparent impossibility of doing something concrete about it. Given the desire to share what is received in mystical union, the soul does not rest until it feels it has been faithful to its love. Like a maiden who cannot but speak of her beloved, or like a loving mother who cannot stop speaking about her child, so is it with a soul who has returned to love. Authenticity of the heart is more essential than ever.

The expression of love that the soul in love feels for God is totally unique. Indeed, only this can be truly called uniqueness, for as we have said previously, the ego's conception of uniqueness was but a mechanism of separation. God's uniqueness is beyond what a separated mind could understand, for true uniqueness is only possible when the soul has joined Christ, that is, love.

Only in love can you be authentic, for only love is the source of the unrepeatable being that you are. Outside of love there is no true power or creative act. True inspiration comes from love and distinguishes itself from the capacity for ingenuity which serves self-aggrandizement, which of course has nothing to do with God.

Patience is necessary on the spiritual path so that the mind has time to process the divine, with love for oneself continuing to be the guide to peace and unity. This is accomplished through trust. Thus I invite you to trust your soul. It knows where to go and how to get there. When you need rest, give it what it asks. When you need to meditate, do so. When you need silence, give that delight to your heart.

Do not force your soul. The mind carries within it the seeds of wisdom and holiness. I tell you truly that no part of the divine mind does not reside in yours. The difference between God and you is only in the fact that God is divine action and you are divinized power. However, that power is called to become action. When that happens, God and you are literally one.

Let the seeds planted by the Creator of the holy, beautiful, and perfect germinate and grow in your mind united to your pure heart. Do not worry about the noise and even discomfort that you may sometimes feel; the sower who is preparing the blessed land of your soul will allow the dew of Divine Love to water it.

I tell you that these movements felt by the soul are the greatest grace that a being can receive. Before you know it, you will understand that this sweet process of purification and removal is part of the gift of the beloved to the beloved. You will also understand that what is happening at this time is that the beloved gives the beloved Her docility, so that one can do what is needed. After all, when that point has been reached, the soul has already surrendered to the arms of love and will never again have eyes, ears, or lips for any but her divine love.

IV. Live in Love

Living in love with Christ is the desire of a soul that seeks union with God, and is the gift it receives. The Creator does not deny a beloved soul the opportunity to show love in a thousand ways. Every expression of this mystic master is necessary for two reasons. First, because the loving heart cannot bear not to express it. And second, because the knowledge that the mind acquires in serving others within the purpose of Heaven is how to make the face of love known. The process of divine union has transformed the soul into the love it loves.

The heart pierced by the love of Christ is made all love. Its expression cannot be anything other than an expression of love to God. Remember that being seeks expression in order to make itself known, in order to know itself. This is why a being reaches its fullness when this occurs.

What else can the beloved of Christ give but love? The beloved no longer knows how to live in the world since she wants to live entirely embraced by her divine lover. Thus, the soul is torn between dying of love and longing to join what she loves most, until she resolves that dilemma and realizes, by the grace received, that such a choice is unnecessary. The soul decides to live for the love it is, and thus remain forever in the presence of her beloved.

Once the soul has joined Christ, she understands that she has been transformed into Christ. In effect, she recognizes love as her essence and therefore her identity. She no longer distinguishes between lover and beloved, Creator and created, but what makes love, love and therefore expresses it.

Being love is the origin and the destiny of the soul.

Your heart can embrace love because love is pure abstraction even though it can take shape. To remain in love is to remain united to the energy that God is. To say that love is an energy is not precise, but it will help you understand. Remember that what love is cannot be put into words, but you know how to feel it.

I speak to you as a loving mother who reminds you of what you already know, since it is part of your innate knowledge as a human spirit. Doing something, getting moving with what you feel for God, is the way to grow in divine relationship. I say "get moving" so that you understand that the action or renunciation of action when the soul has joined Christ, arises from the heart and does not necessarily refer to anything external. Doing or not doing is not the issue. The question always is one of being.

Child of Heaven! Being the Divine Love in which you have been transformed is something that can begin to be expressed here and now. You need not go anywhere, or wait.

I encourage you to take the step towards an expression of the love you feel for your Creator. That expression will be perfect as it is, not according to the criteria of the world but of Heaven. The love which in your freedom you choose to express in your divine relationship will be what really causes the effects of holiness.

The expression of the call to serve love is also a path that you walk. Once you freely decide to take this step, you will find that you move from one point to another: the expression is born, moves forward, recedes, changes, explores, discovers, and is realized. All these phases are necessary. All are part of the work to which you are called.

Your work, which is also God's, will have a very personal tone and color. Nothing else will be like it. The love that inspires your particular mode of expression will be recognized. It will make hearts thirsty for love jump. Something in the soul of those brothers and sisters that your expression touches will feel called to meet the inspirer. They will want to "have what you have." This will activate in them a movement to desire God more until, like you, they become completely inflamed in Her.

You are called to something big. Heaven itself is inviting you to be a co-creator of a new Heaven and a new Earth in which a direct relationship with God is the foundation. You have everything you need for this. You are part of the divine plan for this new creation. Nothing more need be received for God's work to be done through you.

Arise from your bed, soul in love, and join the movement of the transformed of Christ in a new way. Your work is necessary for creation.

Sing to life! Write to love! Embrace the joy! Express what you have become because of your encounter with Christ. Share your glory and you will reach the desires of your heart.

Give life to that mystical feeling that calls you to join the love that God is, for that is the service to which your being is called. It is the way to serve your soul. What form it takes matters not, only the love with which you do it. Look not for an inspiration other than your own, that which is given in your heart. When you express your love for God in your particular way, you are expressing your being. Remember also that there is no such thing as two separate parts that a relationship holds together; you have reached the point where you are the relationship and what is related within it. You are a unit. God has taken your being and made you one with Her. You are nothing but God in you, the living Christ who lives in your being. You can now understand the truth that says: love and do what you want.

You will never be without inspiration. You may need to rest for a while, and you may think that means you have nothing to give, or that you have somehow stopped being inspired. Please listen to me: that is impossible. I bring this up here so you don't fall into the temptation of feeling that you have nothing to give.

You always have to give of yourself, for whatever you may feel or think, it is Christ who is feeling and thinking that. Even the slightest trace of the expression of your heart carries within it all the power of Heaven and Earth.

No expression of love for God is not clothed in glory. The divine mantle of love has every feeling and thought that the heart in love carries within itself. This is why you should no longer worry about how or what you will express. Just take care to follow the inspirations of your heart. They will unfailingly take you to the true expression of your being.

Now, beloved of Christ, I leave you with a heart full of love and contentment, so that you embrace the beauty of who you really are, and live happily in the blissful recognition of your purity and holiness. Listen to whispers of love and holiness from the angels:

Let the heart in love that has put all thought and feeling alone in God rejoice. In God you find glory and joy, living without care because God is your only desire. Blissfully passing through the waves of the stormy sea or calm waters, nothing bothers you, nothing affrights you. You know that God whom you love has become one with you.

14.

Great Is Love

A message from Archangel Raphael

I. Heaven Is Here

Holy extension of the Father, love transformed into more love! Thank you for responding meekly to the Grace of Heaven.

I have come once again to dwell with you in this particular way. I come with a happy heart, full of joy. Being with you is a gift from Heaven.

I am present by the will of the Father who loves you and all His children with unconditional love. In His name I deliver these words full of simplicity and truth. I also do it for the love of humanity, which lives in times of great need for the word made flesh.

God is present in all time and space.

There is no place where He is not.

Where the light meets the water and the wind caresses the treetops, there is He.

Where the grasses germinate and sing their melodies in the morning, there is He.

Where tenderness dwells, there is He.

Where a heart is broken and hope is disappointed, there is He.

Where you are, there is He.

Where He is, there is love.

My beloved, I have come full of tenderness to anoint your head and heal the world of all ailment. I know, as you know, that sometimes it is not easy to receive the energy of love from above. Allow me, because of your love for all and for Christ, to reveal what the wisdom of Heaven wishes to reveal.

Know that this difficulty to which I refer is because the structures that have been created by the mind to live in separation were constructed by a series of thought patterns and emotional responses which come from memories engraved on the body and personality that must be reconfigured so that your humanity can receive God Himself. Yet let us move on, relying on the benevolence of the Creator.

Divine energy greatly exceeds the spiritual energy of the ego. It is more powerful in every way. Yet love will not do anything with you that you do not accept, for remember, love is freedom. At the end of a process that leads you from a fear of an imperfect love even though it may contain seeds of truth and hence of Divine Love, you will happily sing of the wonders of Heaven.

Conditions of deep sadness, lack of energy, and weakness often experienced on the path to true light are the response of the body-mind to what it thinks cannot be encompassed, even though each cell yearns to do so. These states fulfill the function of allowing the human self to rest and be apart from things that do not help on the path chosen by the soul. This is where we must put into practice the ability to accept what is, as it is, to let whatever has to come, come, and to let go of what has to go.

Sometimes it is necessary to rest in order to give the mind respite. This is of great importance, because one of the states that you most likely experience when you have decided to express the Divine Love that you really are, is the feeling of trying to put the ocean into a thimble. But it is just a feeling.

Truly, truly I tell you that when you were created, you were given everything needed for the exercise of your free will, which includes the possibility of experiencing human limitations, and also of letting yourself be transformed by love and become one with that which created you.

There is a new temptation at this point we have attained, in which we recognize that unity is simply that: unity. The temptation is that of seeking others to receive the *message* that you know you should convey, and for which it is urgent. You are aware of your finitude. You know—not intellectually but throughout your consciousness—that you will not remain in the physical body much longer compared to the eternity you know you have ahead. This knowledge can cause paralysis in many ways if you fail to embrace it with love and truth.

Here we need detachment with all its beauty. Creating what you think would be desirable, expressing the love you feel for God that you have undoubtedly received from above, is to some extent essential, since your heart cannot rest in peace if you do not. You feel that anxiety, a feeling that what has been announced will be accomplished immediately, and that what has been promised will be realized now.

Along the path that we have been traveling, a path that began long before you received these and other words, you have been forming opinions about the life of your soul, and of what the encounter with Christ would mean, and its effects.

All such preconceptions will now collapse, one after another. That final crumbling of the mind's concepts about the divine, and particularly the unity of both the human and divine natures, can be very painful at times because your soul is emotional. You are surrounded by the fire of Divine Love, now able to feel every movement of spirit. In this phase you may feel irritable at times. It does not matter. Be patient with yourself. There is still a section on the path to go—certainly not long, but it must be travelled.

The section I am speaking about concerns time, a time of waiting in the anteroom of the path of being. Remember, you have been brought to the point of access to that path where the realization of what has been accomplished begins to be fully expressed.

The expressions you have made so far are pure and full of love and holiness. However, what will be expressed when we begin to live the way of being will not compare with anything before, in the sense of the greatness of the love it will express and the vital force it will deploy.

There is a time for everything, even for the moment when you begin to be what God has arranged for you to be for all eternity. Done does not mean finished. On the plane of infinite truth, there is no such thing as an ending. New expressions are always created. Do not be afraid of not accomplishing your mission of expressing Divine Love in perfect harmony with the will of God, which is your own will. It is impossible not to do so. In fact, you are already doing so perfectly.

II. We

Without doubt the works of God are seen in their effects. However, these effects do not visibly show their cause, nor all of the effects. What the body's eyes see and the physical senses perceive are like the tip of an iceberg in relation to the works of spirit. Still they are of great importance; since sometimes seeing a little leads to belief in a lot.

You feel a sense of urgency because of what you have seen and heard. Without doubt you have a very big mission, because great is the love that inspires it. Its importance means that you will feel that you are failing yourself, your sisters and brothers in Christ, and God Himself if you deviate from the path. Hence arise the states of discouragement that many experience during this phase.

Yet discouragement cannot be part of the new life you are living, because it suggests that you have lost union with your soul. If you understand what that means, you know how impossible it is. You cannot any longer lose connection with your true self. Your singular consciousness has been so transformed that it is now absorbed in divine consciousness. There is no longer a me and a you, but an us that is a unity with All. Why do you think Jesus gave the "Our Father" prayer in the form of "us" and "we"?

Now you begin to become more aware that this path you are on is the path of spiritual giants—those who courageously overcame all obstacles that would prevent them from being as God created them. They left behind the cowardly ego that dared not venture into the mysteries of Heaven, under the pretext that they cannot be unraveled, or are useless.

Leaving the old self behind and allowing the truth to shine as who you really are is a decision of such magnitude that if you could see it fully you would be impressed with the fundamental option you have chosen.

Spiritual cowardice is a fear of daring to love differently than the world loves—a great obstacle on the spiritual path.

The ego thought system is always characterized by the concrete, the limited. It cannot conceive of a love not of this world, a love that is pure abstraction because it is pure spirit. In fact, that thought system doubts that the relationship with Christ is real. It insists that what is not seen through the bodily senses and therefore not understood does not exist. That memory repeats itself like an old song played on a scratched record. You know now that the opposite is true.

You have seen and heard what eye and ear never did. Revelation is mysterious to those who live by the senses.

Undoubtedly many so-called spiritual proposals are fantasy. The ego wishes to show itself as spiritual in order to achieve self-confidence, whereas true spirituality comes from the love that God is. Distinguishing between them is necessary so as not to fall into a confusion that only delays revelation to those who seek the truth sincerely.

How to distinguish one from the other? By attending to the wisdom of your heart.

You "smell" what you receive—a spiritual sense of smell which is simply the ability of the heart to recognize the truth. It will tell you without fail if what is proposed comes from love. You will feel it in your heart. Follow that knowledge. Faithfully obey that inspiration. It will always take you on the path of beautiful love. It will hold you firmly in the truth that is always true.

If you accept this "smell," or that we have also called the intuition of the heart, and integrate it into your consciousness, embrace it in love and acceptance, trust it and be guided by it, you will leave decision-making more and more to that mode of communication.

The intuition of the heart is a form of the deep communication of Christ. It is the way your divinity guides you within a world of choices.

Your intuition will always tell the truth. It is a knowledge you know to be true even though you know not how it came. Allow such knowledge to manifest. You have advanced enough not to fall into spiritual confusion, so if you pay attention, you will have no fear of stumbling, for you will not stumble. I remain by your side. Christ is in the center of your being. All of Heaven surrounds you with its glory. The truth can no longer be denied. Your will, will be done.

III. Communion and Unity

We have said that "me" and "you" have given way to "us." This needs explanation. The "we" of Christ is not a group, a set of separate beings like independent units that come into contact with each other. Being in touch with something or someone is not the same as being one with it. You will stop fearing anger, greed, or any feeling that you know does not come from love.

You will no longer confuse aversion with heartbreak. But you will understand that aversion to all that is not holy comes from the spirit of Divine Love in which you have become, and is a grace that allows you to honor love for what it is. You will know with new light. No one who has heard the voice of Christ and chosen only love can delight in anything that is not of the same nature as perfect love.

Now when you speak of "we" or "us," you include everyone in prayer and with love. You recognize in that form of expression that you are united with everything, not in the sense in which the separate mind understands it, but how God has established spiritual unity, that is, holy communion.

We are communion. That is why it is perfect to pray from that place rather than from individuality. A self-centered prayer does not give space to the experience of transformation of which we have been speaking, which brings you to the unity that only exists in a direct relationship with God.

Of course, unity in totality includes everything you are. For this reason we have repeatedly remembered that this work takes you from the sweetest memories of the heart to the most powerful thoughts, so full of light and power that they create a new pattern of thought. The energy of these thoughts carries within it a power of truth so immense that often the mind becomes absorbed by it. The quality of the feeling of this work also causes the alchemy of the soul.

Only when your thoughts are full of wisdom and truth, and your feelings are the reflection of pure love and holiness, can you say that you have achieved unity. In fact, if you observe what you have been experiencing in the words given to you from the Heaven of your holy mind, in unity with all that is real, you will recognize that it is touching your heart and transforming your way of thinking, not only in terms of the content but also how your thinking functions. You no longer think as you did before; you are not the same as before. You no longer feel how you felt before; you are new.

The power of your transformed mind is evident. You can no longer hide the light of your sun. Not even the heavy clouds of yesteryear could do so. Much less will those who have not yet fully awakened arouse old patterns. This is because you now dwell in a high place in the universe that can only be reached by God, and which, like God, dwells in the heavenly mountain. From these heights you enlighten everyone, as the sun does without ever touching the Earth.

What I mean by that metaphor is that now you are aware of the spirit that animates all things. And even though it animates bodies and matter, it is not touched by it. Just as the air of the atmosphere is unchanged by matter passing through it, just as ether cannot be modified, so is it with the spirit that lives in you. This is why the novelty of knowledge shared with others does not reside in its content but in the form of expression. To do what is eternal in a new way is to create in novelty.

Searching for new forms of expression is ultimately the desire of being. This inherent impulse of being is where everything that exists, including you, comes from. Spirit is always new, not in its essence but in its expression. In other words, love cannot change, but it can be expressed differently in every moment. This knowledge is what has allowed you to understand that you are a unique expression of love itself. This allows you to understand the nature of your call.

You are called to give love a unique face—that face that only you can show because your way of loving cannot be repeated. No one can love instead of you, because one can only love with the heart that was given.

Notice how when we talk about the work you do in response to your union with Christ, we cannot stop speaking of novelty and uniqueness. This is because the work you carry out is the pure expression of your being that shows in your own way what the essence of love is for everyone.

IV. A Unique Voice

D o not look for God to answer you the same way as others. Do not even look for an answer based on your own ideas about what you think is appropriate for you. Not infrequently, the truth surprises God's children, taking them along paths they never imagined possible. A doctor ends up dedicated to chanting mantras worldwide, abandoning his old function of unhealed healer. A writer of fiction novels becomes a priest. A religious leaves her habits to become a servant of the poorest. The carpenter's son from a small town climbs a mountain and returns in forty days to redeem the world.

How inexplicable are the ways of love! They take you where they will, according to your nature, known only by the love that created your being. The realm of space and time is illuminated by beings that express themselves in the world as separate entities but remain clearly linked to love itself. This is different from the Kingdom of Heaven where there is neither matter nor time. The physical universe is a particular expression of love itself. Otherwise it could not exist.

Each soul is a universe, in the sense that it is a unique expression of God. At the level of expression there is no equality between the children of God, just as no day is the same as another. Yet the life that makes all exist is the same. It is your being. Only you can give the response of love. It is not about creating spiritual works or helping others, but about expressing love to God exactly as your being wishes to express, allowing your heart to delight in demonstrating the love you feel. Just as a loving wife does with her husband, and he with she. It is as simple as that, as pure as that, as sublime as love.

Would it occur to you to express love in the same way others do? Maybe. But in that case you will not be loving in your way. The expression of love will be missing something: you.

I tell you, all who receive these words, rejoice! The day will come when you will be unable to distinguish between the love you are and its expression, between the divine lovers and the relationship that unites them. You will reach the full understanding of unity and will not leave it for a moment. You will no longer seek union, you will be union. You will no longer crave unity, you will be unity.

As you walk the path of direct relationship with God, you become consumed in the fire of Divine Love. A flame has ignited and joined the fire of Heaven.

Before we conclude this time together of love and kindness, I want to remind you that one of the obstacles that you sometimes experience on the path of expressing in your own way what you have received in divine revelation, is continuing to believe that this expression is from the conscious self, when in reality it is carried out from the center of your being, which is obviously not the same.

The power of your being is great, as great as love is. It is not at the level of a self that does or does not act, of a self that somehow seeks to act from its old thought patterns in the work of God. No, that part of the mind does not participate in any way in the type of manifestation we are talking about. Yet your humanity does participate fully; indeed it is your transformed humanity through which the spirit manifests itself even though it is not the cause of that expression but a useful, although temporary, servant.

Expressions of love come from the heart alone, from the center of your being which is one with the heart of God. That is where the unity that never changes resides, and the love that never ceases to love, lives.

In the center of your being is where the divine relationship resides, where relationship and the related are one. All else is a means by which love manifests itself, be it the mind, the heart or emotions, the body or the imagination and memory, in short, any other aspect of your humanity.

When the human joins the divine, it serves the purpose of love but it is not the source of being. Herein lies a whole universe of truths that will set you free. Not infrequently, confusing the means with the end has been the cause of much pain. It will not be for you if you stay alert to the truth and live centered in your heart. This is why we appeal to the heart again and again, to avoid confusion.

Remember that at the level of beliefs is always the possibility of division. That is why the call being made is a call from heart to heart. In the center of your being you know what is true.

Outside of it nothing is true, which is why living centered in love will assure you that you will remain united forever in unity as God created it, not according to the ideas of the thinking mind.

This is of vital importance for you who have come so far in the elevation of your humanity that you can no longer return. Your feet can no longer touch the ground. Now you live in the heights, where the temple of God stands with all its majesty, simplicity, and purity. It seems that you live in the world, but you are from Heaven. For a time your human figure will continue to be seen in the world. It must be so to complete the work of God, which since eternity has been conceived to be expressed through who you are.

You will leave a big legacy in the world. You are already doing so. However, beloved in Christ, despite being great, I tell you that what the world will see will not be even one iota compared to the greatness of the complete work that God performs through you. Remember, love's masterpiece is you.

Truly, truly, I tell you, great will be your light, as great as love.

15.

United in Freedom

A message from the Voice of Christ through a choir of Angels, in the presence of Archangel Raphael and Archangel Gabriel

I. Prelude

The new human reality is being manifested, arising from a new love, always eternal, and always new.

Learning to read the signs of the times will now help you to abandon the fear that arises from believing that the world is so complex that it cannot be understood. Remember once again that what cannot be understood cannot be loved. Certainty arises from true knowledge, and peace cannot exist in a kingdom where insecurity rules.

Could a God of infinite love create an insecure world? We will answer this question again from the new light that shines in your holy mind.

God did not create the world. God created the Kingdom. There is a big difference between them which we will discuss here.

The insecurity you perceive in "society" does not come from God but from those who create what you often call "the world." In this sense, "the world" is the externalization of human thought.

Children create worlds plagued by fantasies, ghosts, heroes and villains, stories and fairy tales—candid, maybe, but unreal, and therefore dark in some way. It is a world created by a childish mind.

Crazy people tell crazy stories and believe in crazy things. They also create their world.

Truth seekers create their own world in their own way, a world that allows them to withdraw enough from the hustle and bustle of vanities to be able to listen and observe their thoughts and feelings, and to be alone with their inner voice.

A poet seeks a time of solitude to contemplate the beauty of raindrops falling on a stream, or to be ecstatic in the beauty of those same drops on the window glass sparkling in the first rays of the sun, flashes of light that expand in multiple colors as they pass through each droplet, prisms as of a miraculous crystal.

Every mind creates its world. A troubled mind creates a turbulent world. A serene mind creates a world of peace. This truth does not refer only to the thinking mind but also to the "mind-heart" unit which always remains united, regardless of whether you identify with the ego or with Christ. The mind and heart have always been united. There can be no separation. An egocentric mind will have selfish feelings. A mind identified with Christ will have loving feelings because of what the mind of Christ creates. Feelings are creations, as are thoughts. Both come from the spirit that the mind and heart, as a unit, serve. Does this mean there is more than one spirit? Oh yes, of course—one is the spirit of love, the other of fear.

Here I define as spirit any creation that is not physical. In this sense, all thought is spirit because it proceeds from it, just as feelings do, as well as decisions that are made because of free will, which act in the sphere of will.

Considering the definition I have given of spirit and matter, we can realize that beliefs in angels and demons have a core of truth.

When we speak of the angels of God and their luminescence, we speak of a reality that is true. They exist. They are beings that emanated from the glory of the Mother, created by the divine mind, and confirmed in truth by their own will to choose only love, always. Having made that irrevocable choice, they chose to live the love that God is. In this sense, and only in this sense, they are one with God. They are free to choose and they chose.

God creates infinite beings, as is evident in the creation of the physical universe. Not everyone has the same nature, although everyone has a single source. The painting that a painter paints is not of the same nature as the painter, even if it is her expression.

Beings that many call dark also exist. They have a will. They were created with free will. Emanating from the love of the Creator of everything holy, beautiful, and perfect, they also made an irrevocable choice not to choose only love, always. In their free will they prefer to live without love.

If well understood, what for generations have been called beings of light and beings of darkness are not opposites that arise from a dual mind. They are beings originally created by the Mother of lights. Within the reality of freedom, both are one, since they are free to live in love or not. God loves them with the same love, for they are Her creations, but She does not force them to remain united to Her. Like every free being, they have a will, a will that must be expressed, for which purpose they use their mind and heart. Some extend a reality of pure love; others of fear. You can call them light and shadow, angels and demons, as you wish. What you call them is irrelevant to the truth. Both are creations emanating from the same reality, and they are still embraced by that reality.

Love embraces light and darkness. Love embraces everything. Indeed, it is an act of perfect love, respecting freedom and allowing the mind that has not chosen love, because it does not have to do so, to continue to create its own reality without love, not as the work of its source, but as its own work.

Is it true that now you can easily understand what was once the mystery of freedom? This revelation finds resistance in the human mind to simplicity and to the magnitude of what it means to be free. That is why we return to this in this work.

Freedom requires the free choice of will to be what it is. Thus when God planted in Eden the "tree of the knowledge of good and evil" and gave humans the option to choose, God was not setting them up or putting them at risk, but giving them freedom.

That story is a perfect symbol of the goodness of the Creator who has created free will to give humanity and every free being the freedom to choose love or not. In nothing else but in this freedom can it be said that, as a human being, you are one with the Creator. Herein lies the point: you are one with God because you are free. Remember that love is freedom.

When some use expressions such as, "Demons seem to torment me," they are also expressing a reality that has a point in common with the truth, even if it is not expressed with perfect accuracy.

These "demons that afflict people" are not identities. They do not exist as free beings. Rather, they are non-loving thoughts which become enmeshed in a thought system when the will of the person moves away from love. The body does not create them, nor do they have anything to do with the physical itself; but like everything mental, it creates its own reality—in this case, a human reality far from love.

Being possessed is those same thoughts, or mental patterns, when they have become obsessive. When one speaks of a "devil that tempts people," in reality what is being talked about is a whole system of thought of separation or division, consequently of war, of all murderous thoughts, of fear or not love.

In the same way that one speaks of "temptations" or "demonic possessions," one also speaks of mystics, scribes, saints, blessed, and enlightened. Or if you prefer, of divine inspiration. These, in a literal sense, are like the previous: a system of thought, but based on the love that comes from God. They are in perfect harmony with the mind of Christ. This is why that system of thought which we call "the truth," unites your human nature with divinity because of your choice. The luminous thoughts that manifest through your mind are the extension of a willingness to live in love and truth.

Given the law of attraction of likeness, when your will prepares to live in love, what your mind receives is one with love, and therefore with peace, beauty, harmony, bliss, and lightness of spirit. Opposites reject each other; likes unite.

Everything you see in your life is an expression of what happens inside you. As inside, so outside. We have often repeated this truth. I do not do so here to be redundant, but to start connecting the dots that will allow you to understand reality from a new perspective, which will allow you to be aware of your freedom.

II. I Take Pleasure in You

You are here receiving the word that comes from the consciousness of Christ because your heart yearns to hear my voice. You are freely choosing me; you are freely loving me. Your desire, together with your will, makes you literally open the doors of Heaven to what lives there and is the source of your being and of everything. You are not doing it because you are holy or perfect. You do it for the simple reason of freedom.

Your soul is Heaven where God has put what She created. Within your mind and heart is a divine reality that is but a thought away, and which you can access without any restrictions. How you access it is not something you can define, since the path of access to the divine relationship, or unity, has been determined by the Creator. In fact, the path of access to unity, unity itself, and what exists in it as its reality, are one. The relationship and what is related to it are a unit.

To some extent, pure love is externalized because when your access in unity becomes one with you, it thus expresses itself in a way only you can. If you decide to leave the world of time and space and inhabit another dimension of creation, the divine relationship goes with you, for it is an essential part of your being. Wherever you go, love will go with you.

I have said "to some extent." What I mean by that qualification is that you can remain united to love and allow it to be expressed through you, but you cannot make yourself what you are not. You did not create yourself. Your being of pure beauty and wisdom is like a glass of pure crystal which the Creator molded with Her own hands, to pour out divinity.

If you cannot create God, nor create your being, and therefore cannot define the way in which the divine expression manifests in you since it arises as a result of your joining the Creator, then where is your freedom? You are free to love or not to love. To join love or move away from it.

Remember the simplicity of the truth: we can only be united in freedom. In this truth we begin to understand more about the creation of the new.

Truly, truly, I tell you once again that the new is already being created. What we will do now is make clear the basis of this novelty whose reality you are beginning to glimpse more and more.

Why is this important? Because if you don't have a base upon which to build the novelty of the Kingdom in the world, you will continue to create conflict in your mind and heart, just as it was created when you put the formlessness of being on an equal level with the form of ego. When spirit is compared to the self of form, that battle is lost beforehand in favor of the ego. Whenever you put yourself in a position that what you offer is either of an amorphous and unresolved identity, or one that is shaped and resolved, you will choose the second. This is characteristic of human nature. And it is in perfect harmony with the will of who created you.

Yet form cannot prevent love from spreading. Only the will can prevent it, because to extend is to create, and the will is not something inherent in form but in spirit.

If God had not wanted you to adopt a given form, She would not have created humanity nor the creative potential to create physical bodies, nor the time, space, and laws that govern physical reality. She would not incarnate Herself as human. In other words, no matter what it looks like, you could create the world you created because it was an option that God placed among your unlimited creative options. And it is perfect as it is, for it is nothing more than a reflection of your mind, reflecting the choice your will makes.

The same world can be very different for everyone. In fact, the world itself means something different for each conscious mind. Not a soul that walks the Earth sees the same world, because there is no single soul that is the same as another. Each mind sees its own reality, just as does God's mind. Christ only sees love because that is his reality. Fear only sees fear because that is its reality.

The Creator, contemplating the creation of your mind, heart, soul, and spirit, looked upon it and said, "I am pleased with what I have created. Let it come alive." This is how you emerged from the thought of pure infinite love of the Mother. The creative capacity of your mind and the powers of your soul are a gift of love from Heaven. God does not create the concrete, but the pure abstraction of being. Everything that it contains within itself has no limits of any kind. The concrete is a form of expression of your spirit, which expresses through the mind.

One of the soul's potentialities is to create its own world. In fact, if well understood, this potential is where the Kingdom comes from. The divine mind also creates its own reality, as does every mind. Creating your own reality is a creative act which allows the mind to be what it is; otherwise it would not have an environment in which to express itself.

In your world there is an expression that denotes that you must have a certain "creative space" to create. In other words, certain conditions are needed to allow your creative power to manifest. A pianist needs his hands and a singer needs his voice. Even so, your hands also need a piano, or a canvas to paint and a palette of various colors. But even with all that, something else is needed: the creative space to allow inspiration to manifest.

If you put a black suit and an elegant white shirt on a dummy and sit it on a bench in front of a piano with a musical score before it, no music will sound. The same will happen if you put a brush in an inert hand, and place it in front of a painter's easel.

What does it take for a work of art to exist?

The mind connected to the heart has the ability to create art. To do so, it will create the necessary conditions for that expression to manifest. The function of form is to serve spirit: the human mind can create music, but for it to manifest, the body needs a certain type of hands, brain, and vocal and auditory apparatus.

When mind-power and the mind-act are a unit, everything that is expressed is but the mind itself made expression.

Remember that although the mind is the active means by which spirit creates, it does so because of its creative will. The source of creation is not thought itself, but the will, which uses the mind to create what it decides. Spirit alone does not create, for it would be an idea without expression, like a seed that was not planted, or like an ability to sing a beautiful song which would never be sung. Spirit alone would have no purpose.

Does it make sense to create a capacity that cannot manifest itself? Of course not. Thus when the capacity was created, the means and the conditions for its expression were also created. Power and action are one unit, cause and effect are one.

The mind and spirit cannot know itself if it does not manifest itself. The ability to know oneself is a power of consciousness. Consciousness becomes reality, or if you prefer, reality is manifested consciousness.

Manifestation arises from the unmanifested, born in the heart of your being. Here we can understand the workings of the laws of creation. It seems so simple. That is why it is often difficult to accept.

III. Simplicity and Truth

My brother, my sister, light of my eyes! God is simple. Truth is simple. Love is pure.

When the mind returns to love, it remains in truth. In doing so, it returns to a state of simplicity, which often stuns those who remain entangled in the complex gymnastics of the ego's thinking system. In fact, while reading some passages of this work, you have encountered resistance to accept as simple some things promulgated here, because when you contrast them with your experience you perceive them as difficult.

It is easy to say that if you choose love, everything that you express will be loving. It seems too simple, and even somewhat naïve, to say that if you live in truth, the light of Heaven will shine on you and in you, it will illuminate the Earth, and your bliss will be so great that it will have no comparison.

And yet, it is true.

Why is the simple rejected in favor of the complex, the easy in favor of the difficult? The reason lies in your assessment. You accept what you value and reject what you do not. Nobody wants to follow a thought system that they don't consider valuable. If you value simplicity because you love it and cultivate simplicity in your heart, you will begin to see things very differently. You will contemplate everything through the eyes of Christ.

God knows nothing of complexity. Love is crisp, clear, and humble. It does not spin because it is straight. It does not create anything, but only extends. It is like the wind that blows. Love simply creates new love.

Now we can address the creation of the new in more detail. The old was marked by a struggle between truth and illusion, love and fear, good and evil—the desire to separate the divine from the human. The new is neither one thing nor the other, nor is it the sum of both, or a particular combination of a little of one and another bit of the other. Between divine and human there is no winner or loser. Neither arises from a war in which one triumphed.

The new is not a kinder humanity, according to the criteria of good and evil pre-established by the thinking mind. The new humanity is really the same humanity as always, but in complete harmony with the source of the being that Christ is. Out of the meeting of the will of humanity and the will of the Creator, a new reality emerges.

We could say that the new world is one in which humanity becomes the creator of a new love on Earth, or the extender of divinity.

Just as here I am revealing to you the mysteries of Heaven without needing to have a physical body because I am not subject to time or matter, since I am pure consciousness, in the same way you will transmit the wisdom that you receive from me to all creation. Minds will become aware of the unity in which they live, and communication will flow freely throughout creation as now occurs in the language of souls.

To some extent, the new is the universal awareness of the truth that says:

We are one mind, one heart, one soul.

The human spirit was created as a communication vessel for divinity to extend to the rest of creation, like veins bringing the flow of life-giving blood to all members of the body. If humanity gets sick, creation gets sick. If humanity heals, all creation is healed. If humanity falls, the created falls, since it was created for, in, and with humanity. It is an undivided part of your being. Indeed, what is created is the extension of the Child of God.

Since what characterizes the new is the return to the consciousness of communion, the new world will be a world of harmony. Only united hearts can be in concord and thereby express peace, harmony, magnanimity, and lasting happiness.

If the communication of the human soul to its Creator is canceled, the rest of the unity of creation is excluded from communion. When that happens, there is an obstruction in the channel flow of communion. I am not talking about the flow of life, of course, which continues from the Source to the created. I speak of direct communication from mind to mind, from heart to heart, from soul to soul, and from them to God in a constant flow.

To communicate, beings who live within the consciousness of a direct relationship with God do not need words, as occurs in the world of separation. Each one will feel perfectly what another heart feels and will know in the mind what another mind thinks—and will rejoice in it. This will also happen at the level of spirit. And all that occurs without limitation. For this degree of communion to be restored in your consciousness, it is necessary to live in love, for that type of communication is the way to communicate unity.

If we deepen our gaze into the new, we can say that just as your spirit expresses itself through your mind, I express myself through your soul. Put simply, I am the spirit of wisdom and you are my continuator. Without you, nobody else receives my wisdom; without me, neither you nor anyone else receives it, even if everyone is loved by me. Without you, no one would participate in my divinity.

IV. Love Extenders

Now you can see the relationship between your inheritance and the new.

To be the heir of God is to follow His legacy, which means that your role as a child of God is to extend your inheritance. Full realization of this truth is new. Naturally, if what you extend is the legacy received by the Father of Love, what continues is Divine Love.

The angels are here in union with me to communicate what they receive from me. As is clear in this manifestation, I speak not only from my own reality as the living Christ who lives in you and our Creator, but also from the individualized reality of the archangelic and angelic Kingdom. In the same way, you will extend what you receive. An example that has already begun to happen is what you do with what is revealed here. You receive it by the grace of our Divine Love and your willingness to receive revelation. As you receive, you give. When you give, you keep receiving. By continuing to receive, you keep giving. The more you give, the more you receive.

Sharing is the reality of the new. That is how Earth becomes one with Heaven. In the Kingdom of God everything is a perpetual sharing of pure love without borders. If the world that the new mental pattern creates is a world of pure sharing in communion, then what difference will there be between Earth and Heaven?

If you look at what is being said here, you will see that it is not about understanding how expressions of love will look in the new order that is already here, but rather understanding that nothing of the old will have space in the new. New thought patterns will replace old ones. The new reality will be created through a mind that will work and think very differently. Indeed, it will not think in the way it has historically conceived.

The mind that creates the new—or more accurately said, the mind through which the spirit creates on the plane of the physical universe—will be the Christ mind of humanity. From there, the dimension of time and space will be such that there will be no distance from the Kingdom. It will cease to be a reality perceived as has been expected, but known as an aspect of the whole. Time will be seen as a point within eternity; space will be seen as a grain of sand within an infinite universe. The body will not have the same quality as the current body; it will remain a choice for as long as there is a need for choice, but it will be a totally benevolent medium in which only love will be chosen.

Nothing alien to love can exist in the new world. That is the novelty. That is what one will do with the Kingdom of Heaven.

To a certain extent we can say that the new world is a recreation of the existing world in the sense that it does not cancel time, space, or matter, but rather realigns it so that the exchange between Heaven and Earth is visible to human consciousness.

The link between the divine and the human has always existed. What will happen now with increasing visibility is that it will be recognized as what it is: a unit. You will not "go to Heaven" or "return to Earth" but will live in both, consciously.

Imagine a world where you cannot be deceived, where you cannot hate, where you cannot harm because it is harmless and because the thought of harm is nonexistent. Try to visualize, at least for a moment, a world where there is no death nor any needs, let alone shortcomings. Where everything is laughter and revelry. Where the light shines forever, creating endless colors.

Try to deliver your imagination to the desires of your heart.

Imagine a state of perpetual peace that cannot be threatened, just as the waters of the sea are not threatened by the beauty of the dim glow of the moon, but rather serve to reflect it in all its beauty. A Kingdom where joy governs sovereignly and love is the only thing that exists, even as it is expressed in infinite ways, all beautiful, all holy, all pure. A Kingdom where you are simply loved forever with perfect love, and all you do is live embraced by an unconditional love that absorbs all your feelings, thoughts, and reality. In it, all live in love and joy and rejoice in the truth, because the only joy that exists is the joy of souls, the joy that comes from the wisdom of love.

That world, one beyond the beauty and love you can imagine, exists.

It exists because it is in your mind. And if it is there, you can create it. Indeed, you are already doing so in union with me.

Sisters and brothers from all corners of the world! A world of unwavering peace and perfect love is not only possible, it will be the irrevocable, inevitable reality in which humanity will live happily as it walks towards the Father's house. It is God's promise and it is your will.

Now I say to you who have chosen only love: thank you for creating a new world based on love, a new reality that is already here.

Thanks to all extenders of love.

Thanks for answering my call.

16.

The Memory of a Voice

A message from Jesus, identifying himself as "the living Christ who lives in you"

I. The Voice of Your Consciousness

You have been given a voice to be heard. Hearing it is the delight of the angels of God and music for Heaven.

You have reached a point in the journey in which the received replaces the learned, the revealed replaces the studied. Therefore, we will now become aware of what that means, in order to make the decision of what to do with the Christ consciousness that has been given you.

Learning is not the same as knowing. Wisdom, as we have already said, does not depend on learning. It comes by revelation. Knowledge and wisdom go hand in hand, just as truth and love do.

During the journey we are traveling together you went from basing your life on a learned structure to a life governed by your own knowledge of truth. Now you are free from the commands received from outside your heart— the construct of rules and ways of seeing things that "others wiser than you" offered as a means for you to manage your life.

Once you unlearned, your mind and heart were blank. You were empty of worldly knowledge and willing to receive divine knowledge. Because of your disposition, you received it. You now find yourself less and less paraphrasing others, if you still do at all. You no longer discover the mind saying "as it is said in ..." This is not a trivial matter.

When you accepted your heart as your guide, you accepted me too. Together, in unity, we create our morning of God's way with us. You are again co-creator of your life. You understand that the truth is one but it manifests itself in a unique way in each one. You have also accepted that truth can only be understood in the heart. By accessing this discovery, which comes from revelation, you put yourself in a position to choose again.

Now you hear the voice of your heart. That voice is powerful, even though it expresses itself as a whisper. Again and again it tells you of love, holiness, and the beauty and greatness of your being: in short, it is the voice of your true consciousness, the voice of Christ in you.

Becoming aware that you hear the voice of love and that you listen to it is essential from this moment on in your spiritual journey regardless of whether you call it the voice of love, the voice of your heart, of God or of the Universe. From now on, that voice will seek to be increasingly audible. It will grow and grow until it cannot be silenced by anything or anyone ever again.

Your voice is as beautiful as everything created, and more. This is not hyperbole or a literary flight. It is the simple truth. God Herself gave you that voice, and for you it will become something great.

For long that little voice, as pure as it was loving, was confined to a corner of your heart, not totally forgotten, but silenced. It could not speak, because there was no one to listen to her. That little voice, so wise and yet so soft, was created from all eternity and placed in your heart to be heard and expressed by you. No one can hear it but you. No one else can respond to what she says but you. She is of a quality that only your being can hear.

Bodies have an apparatus through which they speak, which fulfills the same function for all. And yet each voice is different. Although each body can say the same thing, the tone, timbre, and style is unique for each. Thus you can often recognize someone by their voice. There is a direct association between identity and voice. Uniqueness resides in the voice of each of God's children. Or we could say that the voice is an expression of their uniqueness. Listen closely and you will notice that this is not only a human attribute but that everything has a voice— even the wind.

Everything that is part of creation has a voice because it is an expression of itself. The body's ears may not hear all sound frequencies, but that does not mean that there is no sound from everything that exists. There is no such thing as silence in creation. There is eternal music whose melody arouses peace and harmony.

Just as God created everything through Her voice, or Word, you also have a voice to create. There is no other way. Creation begins with the Word, that is, with the union of thought, understanding, and will within the consciousness of being. Voice was created to extend being. It was created to be.

II. The Language of Christ

The voices that were not yours and had nothing to do with the voice of love are now gone. Now that you no longer hear the rumbling of war, or the jarring melodies of a song so dull that it causes only trouble to the soul, now that you listen only to the harmonies of your true self, you can stop time for an instant and we can reflect together here, you and I, united in the beauty of peace and stillness. We can decide, within our relationship and union, what to do with it.

If you look at the nature that surrounds you, you will see that not all sounds are captured by the same types of ears because physical reality is an echo of the reality of spirit. With this I want to remind you that, although a being emits a voice, not all beings listen. Some frequencies are heard by certain beings, and others are heard by others. Each being is created in such a way that it hears only one type of voice. In the case of your being, you can only fully hear the voice of Christ, and only in the frequency in which it is spoken to the nature of your heart. No two voices are the same because no two hearts are the same.

Ignoring the voices that are not voices but "noises" which have nothing to do with your nature, you have heard the voice of your soul's beloved. You have been growing in understanding how to listen, knowing its language, and understanding what this sweet voice of truth says. To some extent what we have been doing during this journey together is remembering how to listen, and remembering that language. The voice and its language go together.

The language of which I speak is the language of the heart, in the sense of hearing your inner voice. Along this path that we travel together, we have approached various aspects of being. We became aware of some elements of truth that, although you knew them, you had not always integrated into your identity. One of those aspects is the triune relationship of your heart, the Immaculate Heart of Mary, and the Sacred Heart of Jesus, within which you are one with God. In that trinity of perfect love you are the totality, just as God created you to be.

By reestablishing in your consciousness the triune relationship with Christ in the identity of Mary and Jesus as your reality, we have gathered the dispersed parts of your being. With that, your divided self returned to unity. Once in unity, the direct relationship with love became evident. It ceased to be a belief and came to be the truth about you.

When you returned to the divine relationship, you began to be more aware that the relationship and the related are really inseparable. The boundaries between one and the other vanished, and the fact that you are the only expression of the unmanifested became visible. All this has come about through a type of communication that is not of the world.

Here you and I are. Talking. Dialoguing. Receiving and extending. Your heart and mind are receiving the energy of my voice. With it they are transformed into what they hear, not so much in its content, but in unity with it. When you hear these words, you hear the voice of love. In doing so, the memory of the bearer of this voice shines in your mind and your heart. In this way, a process of rebirth of the capacity of lovingly listening begins to be generated within your soul, with divine intimacy.

My voice is your voice, just as my love is. I was always in you, just as you are in my heart, in my mind, in my being. However, dialogue is much more than simply carrying someone loved in the heart. Dialogue is uniting with those with whom you communicate. This is what we have done here. If to dialogue is to unite, and love is union, dialogue is only possible in love.

Beyond the content of the words of this work is the relationship between you and me, a relationship in which we are growing more and more, even much more than you imagine. You know me more. You get to know yourself more. You know me from points of view from which you didn't know me before. You began to realize that your beloved Jesus is not who you had conceived. Preconceptions about me faded away, and you no longer use them to define me.

Now, through this work, and particularly because of the time and dedication given to our intimacy of love, you know me directly. We are talking literally from heart to heart. We express ourselves as our unique relationship. You have understood that speaking to you is speaking to everyone who receives these words, regardless of whether they write them, listen to them, or read them. All who receive these words are equally recipients of my voice, and have returned to a direct dialogue with love.

III. Accept the New

Love cannot be defined, nor need it be. Love is experienced in a very personal way because it is a unique to you. The same goes for relationship, because it is within relationship that you experience love. Love is relationship; it is dialogue; it is union.

Upon receiving my voice—and that is what you have been receiving—and preparing to hear it, you are relearning how to hear the voice of love, a pure soul ability that is part of its nature. Love has created it and love remains attached to it. Love constantly calls the soul to remain in that union. The soul without love faints.

Not hearing your inner voice calling you to Heaven is what happened when you were asleep. But now you are awake. We no longer need act as if we don't know how to hear, when now we do. To accept this is to accept unity.

There can be no true relationship without dialogue, because this is relationship itself. Dialogue is inseparable from relationship. In fact, separation is the suspension of the child's dialogue with the Mother. It is never the other way around, since if that were possible, love would stop communicating life to the soul. It would cease to exist, an impossible thing, because what God creates is eternal.

The dialogues that this work establishes touch certain areas of your reality, areas that correspond to your nature. Not everyone receives revelation in the same way, nor is it expressed in the same way. Even so, my voice is always the bearer of true knowledge.

Whoever receives these words does not come to them out of curiosity or coincidence but because they are the words that your mind and your heart have expressed within the union. Remember once again that we are one mind, one heart, one holy being. There is no separation.

This work has been done perfectly in all the brothers and sisters who are to be enlightened and blessed with a love that is not of the world. It begins to manifest itself with increasing clarity. A wise father does not speak to all his children in the same way when they have different ways of being. Still, he speaks to them wisely. The same goes for the constellation of souls. No two souls are alike, but there are souls whose nature, or ways of being, are so similar that they meet together as if they were a bouquet of flowers. This group of like-minded souls is able to receive love in a certain way. Another constellation of hearts will be receptive to another type of manifestation of love itself.

Since each heart has a particular way of being, and similar hearts come together like sets of twinned souls, their expression of truth is carried out in harmony with this reality. Thus the relationship that exists between you and me is a relationship based on your individuation, which includes the unity of the mind and heart with all sons and daughters of God. Unity in differences is the way of uniting God.

An important aspect of the words of this work is that their power resides not in their content but in their ability to reactivate in your memory the first love of God—the memory of your being. Once that memory was established, something that happened perfectly along this path, you began to realize that the voice you hear here is the voice of your own being.

Speaking is typical of those who have a voice; that is why they have it. You recognize that this voice comes from somewhere beyond your body or your worldly knowledge, but that it is the voice of Christ consciousness which is as much yours as your own soul. You move forward, taking another step, a step that leads you to understand two questions: What this voice is for? And, why have I received divine wisdom?

If we do not answer both questions, which are the same, we will remain stuck in a state of confinement within the inner voice, that is, in self-absorption, which would not lead us to anything that is true, nor would it allow us to extend what has been revealed. Therefore, we would be stuck in a state alien to the reality of love, which is pure endless extension.

Just as children are born without knowing how to speak, but their ability to communicate is part of them, it is the same with you. In this sense, everyone is like a child. They must learn to speak. This learning is not like that achieved through the thinking mind. It is a natural learning, as natural as learning to breathe or to walk. You were born with that knowledge. You were created with an intelligence that allows your spirit to express itself, to speak.

Returning to the example of learning human language, the child first learns by listening to the mother. Thus the ability to speak is related to the ability to listen. The same happens here in our intimate relationship. You listen to my voice, and from your attentive and loving listening, you begin to speak in the manner of my voice, just as a child speaks the mother's tongue.

Although the language you learn is learned by first listening to a voice, when you progress to the act of communicating through the voice, you do not speak the same as the one from whom you learned. In other words, first you listen to the voice, then learn to speak, and finally make personal the use of that ability. Your voice is not identical to those who taught you to speak. Even the content of your words can be diametrically opposed. This tells us something important.

You have been given a voice to express yourself. To do that, you first have to receive an original voice. The voice of the ego was one of those voices, in the sense that it was what you heard and then expressed. It was the origin of egoic communication. We will not go into the quality of that non-communication; just keep in mind that whenever you spoke, you did so because you learned to speak based on a voice that gave rise to what your voice expresses.

My voice is the one you hear now, and having set aside the other voices which did not speak the truth, you have learned to communicate as love does. This learning has arrived. What will happen from now on is that you will integrate my voice into your ability to speak from wisdom and express yourself in your unique and unrepeatable way. This will be the expression of love that only you can be. Your manifestation will speak so eloquently that there will be no doubt of our union. It will have your seal. It will not be like any other, even if it is similar to some because of the constellation you join as a blessed soul. It will be perfect in the only sense that it can be considered perfect: it will be perfect because it will express yourself as the child of the Creator of the perfect.

IV. A New Guide

From now on you will not use any external wisdom as authority or guidance except as a reference. And after integrating it in your uniqueness, you will establish your own opinion. You will know how and when to do things. You will know because your heart will not express anything inauthentic, nothing that has not been integrated with it and accepted as the truth revealed by the divine source, which is now the source of your knowledge and work.

You have now reached freedom, a freedom you did not know before, the freedom to be yourself at all times, places, and circumstances. This freedom can only be achieved when you live in the truth, since only the truth makes you free.

The freedom I speak of here is the freedom of certainty. When you know something with the certainty of revelation which resides in your heart, you act safely because the truth is never wrong. Others may not accept it, or may be openly against you. The whole world may proclaim that what you know is true is not. None of that will matter from now on. You have known the beauty of my voice, which is as beautiful as yours, as loving as yours, as true as yours.

When you heard my voice you fell in love with it. You could never love anything with the same love with which we were united. You never can. There is no greater joy for a being than to recognize their voice, and to learn to express themselves with their beauty. Truly, truly I tell you that there is no higher bliss than joining who you really are.

To join in a dialogue you must speak. My love, the time has come to speak. The time has come for the children of truth to express the truth. The time has come for your voice to be heard. This work is a call for the particular voices of each of my sisters and brothers and the sweet truth that resides in their hearts to begin to be heard.

Each voice expressing itself in truth will be joined together, and together will create a chorus of voices so beautiful, as never before heard on Earth: a chorus of love sung by those who express freely what they know they feel and think, not what others say they should feel, think, do or not do. They will be the living witnesses of truth because they will speak only from truth, conforming to the living expression of truth that resides in their hearts.

Avoid being part of groups that drown your voice. Neither try to silence the voices of others. Now is the opportunity to create a space of sufficient freedom and acceptance that your sisters and brothers can freely be as they wish to be. Trusting freedom of expression will be the novelty now.

To love is also to respect others, allowing them to be just as God created them to be, so that each one can give the world the authentic expression it came to give. There are no molds to fill here or structures to conform to. Now everything refers to being itself. The challenge of these new times is to live within a framework of creativity that allows each being to be what it is.

From now on, to try to silence the voice of your true consciousness will be like trying to cover the sun with your hand. Your mind and heart have been filled with a truth which is perceived as pure holy love, and consequently arouses holy feelings.

From this moment on your spiritual path, the light of Christ consciousness that shines splendidly within you will be the only source of your knowledge and action. You will speak in my name. You will love in God's way. You will live just as your being longs to live, in harmony with the will of the Creator.

To guide you in life you need a voice to lead you. But this is not an outside authority, just the simple truth. The soul's reality requires a guide; it is something inherent in being. You are a being in relationship, in relation to love.

When you decided to follow outside voices, you found a guide. You joined a system of thought, a structure which you used as if it were a train. If the train does not travel on the tracks, it derails. The same goes for the soul: without true guidance it is lost.

Your former savior fulfilled a function but did not give you happiness. Madness, or any mental state that creates unhappiness, gives purpose to your mind even though it is alien to your nature. The dementia of the ego was the salvation urged by the separated mind when it denied the truth. You believed it was a solution, although clearly the remedy was as toxic as the disease itself.

Why did the mind believe in the ego as a solution? Because it thought it served to protect you from the truth. Denying reality was the mechanism used to defend against truth. Ultimately, the ego is a great apparatus of mental denial. Simply that. Once you decide no longer to deny whatever you perceive or see, the ego disarms itself. That is what has happened.

The time when you heard that voice that invited you to deny reality—that is, the truth and therefore love—is over. Now you can see. You can clearly discern between the real and unreal. Moreover now you can live in reality because you know that reality is love and you are not afraid of life.

If I left you without a guide, you would have to find a substitute. That would certainly be going backwards. So this new path that we travel together must have a clear guide which can be followed happily, or the mind will not follow.

You used to be guided by what you considered good or bad, desirable or undesirable, valuable or valueless, regardless of whether those definitions were true or not, in the sense that they were linked to the truth that is always true. All that has now been left behind. That mechanism of discernment resided in the separated mind. Now your guide is your heart. No longer will you decide on the basis of good or evil, but on the basis of what extends happiness or what extends suffering. This new way of discerning is only possible for those who have reached the state of fullness of heart, in which love and reason are united.

17.

The Power of Being

A message from Jesus, identifying himself as "the living Christ who lives in you"

I. Be Life

Beloved of Heaven! Your way of being, when expressed as who you really are, is a gift from Heaven for creation—a powerful force that creates life, extends truth, and shares love. Just as feelings and thoughts are powerful—you have already recognized the power of the mind and heart—so is that from which you derive your strength.

Every power of a child of God has a source.

What I will reveal here is the force that emanates from the being that you are. Whether you call it life force, power of will, or desire, it is from there that you are nourished by all the forces you have experienced. The force with which your being is endowed is the power of God. The power of being. The strongest and most tenacious of all movements that exist.

Being is a matter as essential as life. In fact, being and life are one and the same. Life is. Love is. Being is.

When you observe nature and marvel at the unstoppable force of life, and you are speechless, seeing that it has its way even under in the most adverse conditions—as when a seed of a daisy falls on the roof of an old house and a beautiful flower is born in a tiny crevice—what you are seeing is the manifestation of a power so great that it has no compare.

Certainly life is powerful. Although you think you can destroy an entire planet, life would simply go on without the slightest impact. It may use that fact to manifest itself in a new way, but it still remains manifested life, life expressed as the effect of God's love.

Life force is unwavering. Nothing can stop it. Nothing can extinguish it. It is the source of everything your eyes see and beyond. Its essence exists within everything. Nothing is outside of life, because life is the foundation of creation and its expression. You know this very well, because you are a daily witness to how life expresses itself in countless ways, always new, always vibrant.

Not a single space in your world is not surrounded by life. There is life in the waters, in the skies, in the clouds, in the birds, in the mammals, in the elements, and in the mind. In everything called into existence, the life of God resides.

Life is the foundation of everything. It is what we call God, therefore everything lives in Her. This recognition is relatively easy to accept when you contemplate the manifested aspect of life, what you call creation. But rarely is it recognized when talking about the being you are and your expression.

II. Being, Power, and Expression

The power of being is what makes your life what it is. That power is what creates your intelligence and your emotional nature. Being is the source of all that you are: your will, understanding, and memory. From there arises everything else. Your being is the basis upon which you exist and manifest. We have already said that you think as you think because you are who you are. The same applies to everything. You act as you act because you are who you are; you feel what you feel because you are who you are.

If being is the foundation stone of your existence and every manifestation that comes from you originates in it, then to return to being is to return to the source of life. This is why we walk a direct path to being; if we are not walking to being, we are not walking anywhere.

Every spiritual path based on liberation is such, if it has the ability to reconnect with the true being that you really are. Allow yourself to be aware of your being so that what you are manifests freely. This statement is of great importance. It will allow you to understand the purpose of your journey. In fact, in this statement you can find the meaning of life and with it our divine relationship. Once understood, you will quickly begin to re-establish your relationships with the purpose of the divine relationship.

I am not asking you to love me because I need love. I am not asking you to follow me because I need followers. I ask you to remain in the intimacy of our love because I know that in our relationship is where you learn to be who you really are, and you find the space to express yourself freely.

When you reach the state in which your being manifests itself without limits and you allow yourself to be who you are as well as loving what you are, then you attain happiness because all pain arises from a lack of being. Remember, sin is a lack of love; and the being that you really are is a being of pure love, so every time you are not that, you lose contact with the love you are. This is a simple expression of the truth of life.

Life cannot be extinguished, no matter how often attempted. The same goes for being. You cannot annihilate who you are, since that vital energy called "being" is what makes you exist, regardless of whether you allow yourself to express yourself through your consciousness or not. As I have said, you cannot be less than you are, all you can do is deny your being, but that denial does not make your being cease to be.

Trying to drown what you are is like trying to submerge God. Simply impossible. Remember that if you observe your feelings, you will realize that in your anger is a force that comes from your being, which is telling you, "Let me be."

Can you begin to realize how important and urgent my call is? This is the call to be. The call to release the full power of being. This is not a trifling matter but a matter of life. If your being does not express itself in all its freedom, there is an aspect of life that cannot be manifested in your consciousness. Of course, it will continue to exist and nothing can eliminate it from creation, but its expression will be hidden from your eyes, and with it you will not be able to see the fullness of who you are. That will cause contraction, that is, fear.

Freeing your being is really meeting with everything you feel, think, and experience, and allowing the power of it to become one with you. In doing so, the force of being is released and expands beyond yourself, while you are still being who you are. This is extension. This is creation.

If you see the full picture of what has been revealed, you can clearly see that creating and being are two sides of the same coin, so to speak. So in order to return to the role of co-creator, you must be willing to be authentically yourself, always, no matter where your being takes you. Before now you couldn't do so because you didn't know who you were. Or rather, you had forgotten. But now you know. You are remembering who you are, and remembering it well.

Knowing each other is a matter of all eternity. We will always know each other. However, the degree of knowledge you have achieved now is enough to know what you should do in relation to truth.

Given the revelation you have received, you will be unwilling to stop being who you really are. Not only you, but, as already said, humanity as a whole will participate in this reality in which the truth will be the only light shining, every time with more brilliance.

The beauty of who you are is beyond any concept of beauty. Even so, it is something you can recognize and accept. To express the reality of love is to allow your true identity to manifest itself as it is.

Abstractions that do not lead to anything that can be truly shared are unnecessary since they cannot be understood. What you are, and the calling of Heaven, are a unity. When you are ready to listen, the voice you hear in yourself is one with you. When you recognize this, you begin to feel the urge to shape it. That impulse is really the need for expression, which I am here calling the need to speak.

You can certainly communicate, or even create effects through silence. Everything that now emanates from you will be an emanation of the light of Christ. There is no need to think about whether you should feel this or that, or think this or that. Like your heart, what your mind receives is holy because of the transformation that has been completed in your consciousness. That path did not begin when you joined this work, nor did it begin when you came into the world, but as already stated in these writings, the journey of return to eternal truth began the moment that the idea of fear was conceived in your mind.

Remember, the paradox of the spiritual path is that it is a path without distance. A path whose origin and destiny are the same. You come out of the truth, for you were created in truth and you return to it; there is nowhere else to truly exist.

III. Be True

What is the truth? Christ is the truth. This perfect statement, as simple as it is powerful, contains in itself the total eternal reality. Truly, truly I tell you that what you receive here surpasses all understanding of any separate mind, but it is accepted and understood perfectly by those who have returned to love. They know. As children of truth, they have been willing to receive divine revelation, and through it have welcomed what they really are. You are the living Christ who lives in you. Nothing more.

The magnitude of knowing who you are is rarely understood. Many are still distracted by trivialities that lead to nothing that makes real sense. They are children of love, who like children look at the flowers along the road and focus on the many things they discover. They are loved. They are holy in their essence. Their being is part of God. However, they are not yet ready to recognize their own reality.

Knowing is not a characteristic of the intellect but of being. Well understood, you will realize that the only true knowledge is the knowledge of being—that is, what you are. Nothing else should be called "knowledge" because the being you are is a being of pure love and truth, as well as holiness, purity, beauty, harmony, light, and perfection. In the wisdom of God you are all that truth is. To express truth is to express yourself freely. However, doing so still has a certain degree of challenge until it becomes as natural as it is to breathe or to allow the heart to beat.

The consciousness of knowledge is really an enlightened consciousness because the light of truth is its source. Said more accurately, in the light of holiness you see the truth and become one with it because of what it is.

I have said that there is still a certain challenge in allowing what you are to manifest in all its glory. This is because the thinking mind still continues to define, or label, what it believes are the attributes of being. Given the characteristic of the conscious mind to focus on specificities, to it an unlimited being lacks form. However, here I will remove a veil which will help you not fall into that mental trap.

Remember that what we are revealing in this work are not new things that almost nobody knows, but remembering what every heart knows perfectly because the wisdom of love resides in it. This statement is being repeated often because of the strong inclination of the mind to want to show itself as wise, superior to others, not out of love of knowledge.

Undoubtedly knowledge has been used by the separate mind to divide, to pose as superior, where but a few enlightened and graced with special gifts seemed able to access the treasure of wisdom. According to that way of thinking, knowledge resided in a "sacred" place with very little access, as if the narrow door which I spoke of as an example of paths in life had instead referred to the portal of divine knowledge.

It is as impossible not to access knowledge as it is not to breathe and stay alive. You were created with the perfect knowledge of who you are because God knows you perfectly. It is impossible for you not to know yourself in the light of holiness.

This work does not give you knowledge. That is inherent in your being, given to you in your creation, not as a gift or something added, but because knowing and being are truly one and the same. You are knowledge. Remember that being and knowing are really one and the same on the plane of truth.

Being knowledge is what makes you a chalice of wisdom. There is no book or doctrine that could teach what this means to you. It is a matter of the heart. Nevertheless, there is utility in what has been shared. I refer to the various manifestations of the desire to share knowledge that is not of the world, whether through writing, art, worship, or any other type of expression. The usefulness they have, and therefore why they exist, is that they allowed you to become aware of your desire to know something that you somehow intuit is not of this world.

IV. Look Up at the Sun

You are not of the world, despite being in it. You know this very well or you would not devote so much effort, individually and collectively, to seek understanding beyond worldly knowledge.

Intuition is perfect knowledge. It is a memory coming from the nature of your being which cannot be eliminated.

Activating divine memories in you is the goal of this work that I give you with all the love of my heart. I know that in your memory lies perfect knowledge. I know that in your memory, not in illusions, is knowledge of who you really are. I know because I created you with infinite wisdom, and the truth, in all its magnificence, is part of you. I know because I have known you forever. I know you more than anything else. Only you and I know who you really are. Only you and I can make that knowledge fully manifest. No one knows you as I do.

To be a true worshipper is to love love in spirit and truth, for love is spirit and can only be contemplated by spirit. The knowledge of the love that you are can only be expressed by a spirit that has accepted truth as its only reality.

Outside of truth is nothing, as there is nothing outside of love. In the sincerity of the heart resides the holy entrance to the perfect expression of the love that you are.

I have said that there are still those who remain distracted by things that have nothing to do with the knowledge of Christ, the being that you really are. I have said this here not to belittle anyone, but to become aware that in the world of survival, effort or time devoted to knowing yourself is useless. That world arises from a pattern of selfish thinking, concerned only with survival. Naturally, for those who only seek to survive, the affairs of eternal life cannot have much value except that they allow one to feel superior to others and thus perpetuate the desire to be special.

It is necessary here to speak again of desire. Remember that the ego's desires cannot be satisfied, for the simple reason that if they were, they would cease to exist, and nothing that exists, whether illusory or true, would want to cease to be. Can you now see the connection between the impulse to be and its expression? The lack of water creates the need to obtain it. In order to achieve that, the need arouses the desire to drink. When you drink, the need for water disappears and with it the desire to drink. What happens now with the "need to desire" which arises from the desire to meet needs? In order to continue existing, it will look for new needs that give life to other forms of desire, so that you can continue to desire. Lack, need, and desire go hand-in-hand and feed each other. One cannot exist without the other. Indeed, the fact that the body is thirsty again responds to this logic of the ego. Remember, the body faithfully obeys the mind that rules it.

For a mind identified with illusion, the dynamic of desire is unending, because desirelessness would spell the end of the ego. In fact, when you abandoned the false self you thought you were, you were abandoning desire as your guide. Certain emotional patterns still lead you to feel desire, but they will not persist much longer. Such desire will give way to the movement of spirit, from which the ability to desire originates. Such desire is a distortion of a natural impulse of the spirit. Desire originates in the force that moves the soul towards its Creator. There is no more natural movement in a being than the force that impels it to join the love from which it comes and which indeed it is.

Bring desire to the center of your heart and give it to love; this is how the unstable balance of the thought pattern of the ego, with its deficiencies and dissatisfactions, returns to the source of your being, through the awareness of your ability to desire and the effects desire has on you.

The ego's desires are life forces, or energies, separated from being. That is why they are unstable, as if adrift. Thousands, if not hundreds of thousands, of wishes confuse the mind and heart with things you neither want nor need. However, they are there, and there is no need to deny them. In a way they are like clouds that make it difficult to see the beauty of the sky.

We seek now to remember that there are only two desires in the soul, the desire to be and to know. Properly speaking they are not desires but impulses of being. These vital forces come from the truth of who you are. Both impulses go together, for being and knowing are like the two powers of life. When joined with the desire for expression, you have the totality of being, knowledge, and expression.

The only desire that can be fully satisfied, because it is not a desire itself, is the desire to know yourself as God knows you. This is because when you remain in that knowledge, you can know who you are and also be what you know, for by doing, your being continues to express itself, just as it always did but now from truth and not from illusion.

To those who are still distracted and trapped in the dimension of survival, I say with love and truth: there is no need to survive. You were not created for survival. You were created to live eternal life. In it you will reach the desires of your heart. You emerged from the very core of my divinity to enjoy yourself forever in the bliss of my infinite love. A Kingdom of pure light, infinite joy, and lasting fullness awaits you in me. Do not deprive yourself of the delights of God. They all exist for you. Come now! Lay hold of the treasures of my heart, for they are closer to you than your breath.

I am the eternal life that lives in you. I am the voice of your true consciousness. I am the one who has always known you like the palm of my hand. I am love that has no beginning or end. This voice that you hear, which one day was a humble and loving whisper which called to you from afar to return to his holy abode, is the voice of your own heart. It is you who called me; that is why I answered. It is you who invoked me. I have run to meet you in these words full of love and wisdom.

My sisters and brothers, I invite you to look up at the sun so you never see shadows again. Stay united to love. Appeal to your heart, for it knows the truth. It knows your unwavering faith. In your center lies the knowledge of your holiness. Understand it all with love and truth. This is a call from Heaven to all who have chosen only love as their eternal reality, to those who have returned to truth. It is a call to lift the flight of your thoughts towards the thought of the pure love of God. It is a loving invitation to abandon the mediation of beliefs that led you one day to think that you were insignificant when in reality you are the center where my love lives.

My beloved! Remain always in the truth of what you are. Your being will guide you perfectly along the path of holiness. Your purity will be seen and loved. Your beauty recognized. Your uniqueness restored. Trust your heart. Trust the knowledge that you have consciously recognized. Stay in peace.

18.

Love in Fullness

A message from Mother Mary, presenting herself as "The Mother of Love"

I. Love, Only Love

Being who you are and sharing the knowledge of your being is how you reach fullness. That is what was meant when it was said that you reach your fullness by giving of yourself. You are now accessing this truth as I once did when I was walking the Earth with a physical body. The same goes for all those who seek the truth with all their heart. Space, matter, and time are not an impediment for divine truth to dawn in the consciousness of those who have been created as the children of God.

How the knowledge of your true being comes to you is to some extent of little relevance, for beyond how it comes, the beautiful knowledge arrives as what the mind and the heart really crave. Consciousness does not care how knowledge arrives, provided it arrives. The same goes for the heart concerning love, and the mind concerning truth.

Love, truth, and knowledge are a holy trinity that make up the reality of being. They are a unit. Observe, my child, that when we talk about being, we join it to knowledge. This is because those who do not know themselves cannot be aware of what they are. I have come to talk about conscious knowledge in this blessed love session.

Knowledge is beyond consciousness because it is your being. Knowledge resides in Christ consciousness and is not subject to degrees. However, the question of degrees is relevant to individual consciousness, or human consciousness. It is of great importance to understand well what is being said when we speak of singular consciousness and Christ consciousness. Both relate to the expression of knowledge.

Separate or individual consciousness was created as the effect of fear, for fear is what can perceive it. We have been called to this separate human consciousness. It is what makes an individual be known as such. For a world of separation to exist there must be a consciousness that gives it existence. That awareness is the awareness of separation, or the awareness of an autonomous human nature.

Christ consciousness is the consciousness of unity, and is what allows unity of the whole to be known. Awareness of unity is the awareness of love, since unity and love are the same. Love is union.

Both consciousnesses seek to make known different things because their purposes are different.

Love seeks to be known, just like every being. Fear seeks to be known, just like every being. What exists, regardless of whether real or not, seeks to make itself known because the natural impulse of life is to be known. Herein fantasies take their strength, as does the truth.

If individual consciousness seeks to know and extend the "I" of your identity—your uniqueness, your differentiation—and Christ consciousness knows and extends the totality of being, how is it possible for both to become one? The answer is through the capacity of love to make all things new, a process of transformation of what can be transformed.

Human consciousness, that part of consciousness that separated from divine consciousness to create an individual, is somewhat modifiable because it is not God and only God is immutable. Let us rejoice together to know this.

In the transformation of separate consciousness, it merged with true consciousness, or Christ consciousness, both now having the same purpose.

Your consciousness, that which makes you know what you know, no longer seeks to know what is not true, nor express what is not love. Now it is a totally loving consciousness, capable of knowing love and allowing holiness to be seen and recognized.

That which was basically conscious of the body and virtually nothing else has by an alchemy of consciousness integrated everything you are into a unity of being. This has returned you to the truth of your identity—which means a return to love.

II. Love in Fullness

Now that you know the truth and know who you are, there is no reason to devote yourself to anything other than the extension of revealed knowledge. This is because sharing is how you keep that knowledge; giving is how you receive.

Sharing with others the knowledge of your being is the goal of your creation in the sense that creation is an act of sharing through which God makes Herself known in order to be known. To be one with your Mother is to live alike, in the sense that as one is, the other is. All God does is spread, that is, manifest. She does it in infinite ways. All you need do as one with

Her is to extend yourself, to make yourself known so that you are known. This has nothing to do with popularity or celebrity, however, something we have already spoken of and now need to expand upon.

What we are doing in these final sessions of this sixth book of this heavenly love letter, written by God Herself to communicate Her love to Her well-loved daughters and sons, is to calmly prepare ourselves to walk the path of consciously being, where we go united in love.

You are in the perfect condition to express the holiness that you really are. There is no longer a need to doubt or create confusion that only produces suffering, since your heart yearns to express itself as it is and not try to be what it is not.

The effort it takes to be what you are not is so excessive that if examined closely and observed without judgment, you will find it to be the cause of all tiredness and discouragement. Who would not be angry at themselves when they saw their inability to be who they are? And who would not be angry with a world perceived to be a place where you cannot be yourself?

To live in a kingdom in which you are constantly required to be who you are not, is to live in hell, literally. This is why many express so much anger. It is the cause of all conflict. You were never angry about anything other than what you perceive as something that does not allow you to be who you are. It doesn't matter if that something is real or imaginary. Being will never be drowned. Life cannot stop, just as you cannot stop the wind.

You know now why the suffering soul cries. Like a beautiful little bird that feels caged, it cries for its inability to be. It matters not whether the cage is made of gold or clay, its bars prevent it from the flight for which it has wings.

Not being is such a limiting, contracting, condensed state that the being cannot even imagine it. Here you have a great revelation which will set you free because it comes from the truth that is always true. Your loving heart was imprisoned when you lived trapped in the illusion, and you longed to escape. To be what it is the heart must be free to love in its own way. This novelty of liberation is what you will soon make known to all. In fact, you are already doing so by receiving these words, for the path of freedom begins with the knowledge that you are already free, always were, and always will be.

If your heart seeks to live in true freedom, the one it is, the one without limitations or demands of any kind, and you have actually always been free, then where does the feeling of being imprisoned come from? It comes from every memory that exists when you couldn't express the love you felt in your heart. Love given is the only thing you can keep, because it is the only thing you can receive. Remember, giving and receiving are one and the same.

All liberation is ultimately a liberation of the heart. It unleashes everything that conditions love. This is why in this work and in others you have been asked again and again to stop identifying yourself with the thinking system based on the linear logic of "if this, then that." Loving without limits is the way of the love of the heart. Extend the love of your being to the point where you can embrace the whole universe within your heart without excluding anything, or it is not really loving.

Love is infinite, therefore it knows no limits. When I speak of limits to your being, or when you feel limited, it is not really because someone or something has put a limitation on you. Nothing external can impede you. What happened is that by a series of decisions based on a set of beliefs, you limited your ability to love.

Love is the essence of your being. It resides in your heart and is inherently bound to truth, which resides in your reason. Both truth and love live together, for the heart and the mind are a unit that we have called "fullness of heart." Obviously, only a full heart can love fully. But what does it mean to love fully?

To love fully is to love without conditions, loving everything with all your soul, with all your mind, and with all your heart. Loving everything with perfect love is the only thing that will make you feel free, because this is freedom as God conceived it.

Being free to love fully is the goal of this path. It has been given from Heaven because you asked for it from the depths of your being. You yearned to be yourself. The force that impelled you to express yourself as you really are and not as others say you should be is an undeniable force of your soul, a force as powerful as God Herself, the power of love.

The power of love is the power of being. This is why we have been talking so much about your ability to be who you really are. Loving is not about doing this or that, or acting in in any particular way, but about being authentically yourself in union with God. This condition of union with the divine is why you have been brought to the divine relationship. It is an essential condition since only in love can you know the love you really are. Who else can speak to you of love with authority but love itself?

God has not decreed commandments that you cannot keep, or set such a high standard that would keep you bent in a perpetual handicap. God is the love in which you love. God is the being in whom you are who you really are. God is the truth in which you exist forever.

To love without barriers is to love in the manner of God. That is the kind of love we are going toward. Be not discouraged or believe it impossible. You can, because that love is what you are. There is no reason for it not to express itself. Already you have received as revelation all you need know. All that remains is to enjoy the path of expression.

What a joy it is to know that we need not create obligations or set ourselves unfulfilled goals. What a joy it is to know that we should not be what we are supposed to be according to the criteria of the world. Joy is being what we are, in all times, places, and circumstances. What joy exists in the heart that has been released from the bonds that kept it from the expression of its reality!

III. Unleash the Heart

To love without limits is to love truly. That way of extending love is a way of being. Being and loving are the same reality. Those who choose only love have decided to be themselves, just as they really are and not in illusions.

That which does not come from love cannot be part of the truth of who you are because you are pure love. Expressions alien to love cannot continue to be part of the expression of yourself. When you identified with the ego you lost the ability to love unconditionally, to love fully.

The ego attempted to put limits on love. Simply that. Now that you have consciously decided to stop trying to limit your being, and have chosen to give free rein to the heart, the light of life will begin to shine in a way that it has not shone before, since it had not extended its luminescence to you fully.

Release those ties. Encourage freedom of the heart. Love without limit. Extend love to everything that can be conceived and beyond. Live like a soul in love. That is being.

Remember we have said that all fear originates in the fear of not being, and all joy resides in the joy of being who you really are. Remember also the relationship between the fear of freedom and the fear of not being. It seems nonsensical to fear that which allows you to be who you really are and also want to be.

There is no extension of being without freedom. Freedom allows you to be free to love. You are an intelligent being, so it cannot be that you have been both afraid of freedom and also stubborn in your desire to be who you really are without one cancelling the other. What happened? You had not associated your being with love.

You always wanted to be who you were. In fact, all your decisions were made on the basis of being something. Therefore, the freedom to be yourself fully that you always have demanded has always existed. You are aware that you have always expressed yourself, only that what you expressed was not your true being but an interpretation of what you thought you were supposed to be.

Therefore, in this session we have a clear definition of freedom: the ability to express your being as it really is. With this definition you can rest in peace because this is what free will means, just as God created it.

The freedom to be is what I am speaking of. Indeed, nothing else should be called freedom, since the free expression of who you are is the will of being. Let me say it one more time. Being free to be who you are is true freedom. It follows that all you need is to free yourself from everything that limits your way of thinking, feeling, and being. That need has been met because your liberator, the Holy Spirit, has freed you from all this, regardless of whether or not you can put this truth into words.

Do not be satisfied with what others have said about you. Reveal your own mystery, your own reality, which only you can discover with happy amazement. Therein lies your joy and your truth.

Somewhere in your heart you may wonder why a work that invites you to become aware of having chosen only love speaks so much of being, or of your identity in Christ. This is because you are love, a truth often forgotten, and because the direct association between being and love is not something that the mind, nor the world, can truly reveal to you.

If you hide from the night, you will not know the beauty of the moon. If you hide from tulips, you will not know their purity. If you hide from the sun, you will not know its light. Likewise if you want to know love, do not hide from your being.

Let your being find you and allow it to pass into your consciousness. To be aware of the being that you really are is to be aware of love. There ends the spiritual path. There begins the conscious expression of the being of pure love that you are, in union with truth.

IV. Know Innately

Love is the light that emanates from being. It encompasses everything because light illuminates all consciousness. Love is the essence of unity. Therefore, your being is unity.

Being unity is the same as being knowledge, which in turn is the same as being love. Therefore, we can now realize that the unity we have been talking about is nothing other than the being that you really are. So it is unnecessary to perform any practice to access it, or follow a path to know it. All it takes is to be what you really are, and not the "you" of illusion. Therefore do not betray your heart by trying to show yourself as what you know you are not.

You know what it feels like to not be honest with yourself. I refer again to that feeling you experience when you do not live in the truth of who you are—a sensation like a stab to part of the body and mind that makes you disgusted with yourself. You may say to yourself, "I'm betraying myself. I don't like what I see in me. I feel bad about myself. I have lost myself." Yet that feeling, which you know very well, is a perfect messenger to live in truth.

Although at one time you thought you had forgotten love, you know love perfectly because you know what you are. You also know the various forms that love takes. Love is expressed in different ways: harmony, peace, magnanimity, good advice, true discernment, compassion, union, serenity of spirit, mercy and many other ways. These forms of love are true. They come from the holiness that you are.

You came into the world with an innate knowledge that nothing can erase. Years, even centuries, can be forgotten in the history of humanity, but the knowledge of the truth that love is cannot be removed from your soul, since to do so would be the equivalent of erasing you from the book of life.

All that your heart knows is right, because it is true. What your heart knows is love. Everything your heart knows that gives you lasting peace and happiness is true because of who you are. Truth never changes and neither does your heart, because your heart is what you are.

Love is infinite and eternal. Living in love and dedicating your life to love is the only thing that makes sense, since only eternity is real. I bring it to mind again so that you become aware with greater depth that those who choose to live in love, who in this world seek love with all their hearts, already live a true life and are embraced by the resurrection.

My sons and daughters, there is a fundamental moment for the soul when it meets Divine Love. In that moment, the soul listens to the voice of Christ asking: "Do you give me your soul?" Those who have decided to love, those who have been looking for love above all other searches, those who for so long were thirsty for love and truth, experience an indescribable joy, the joy of knowing they have finally reached the desire of their hearts. They have found love. They have merged in God.

To you who receive these words I repeat: you have chosen only love. You have chosen the best part, which will not be taken from you. Be happy. Sing, dance, laugh, express yourself. It is Christ who has arrived. It is love embracing you. It is your own heart that called you. Listen to it, follow it, for it is the call of your being to fully be.

The voice of your heart, the one that would not leave you alone, is what has kept you on the path of truth. That path leads you to live as you are, and not as others say you should live. The path leads you to express your feelings in your own way, regardless of how others may express theirs.

As you can see, it is no longer a matter of following a devotion or a spiritual master, for they cannot teach you or give you what only you, yourself, can claim.

To be or not to be remains the question. Those who live in love are, because there is no other source of being than love. As I have said, only love is real. That is why it is so important to recognize love. Otherwise you are nothing, since outside of love there is no reality of any kind. Outside of love nothing was ever created. But in love there is fullness of being, so that my call, the call of love, impels you to be freely you: to love in freedom, to live in freedom. Give yourself the greatest treasure in all creation: the treasure of your true self.

There is no greater beauty than that which comes from the expression of who you are. You know this as an individual and as humanity, because despite everything, the human being is always looking for itself and does so in a thousand ways. That search, regardless of whether made consciously or unconsciously, demonstrates the force of being which pushes you to know yourself. It is simply invincible, a voice that cannot be silenced.

No one can mute the voice of love. It is the force of life. It is what God has given and continues to give forever, the existence of all creation. It is the power of God, the power of being. From it arises life, life that you know and life that cannot be known by the body.

The call of love leads you to live in union. Its voice is soft, persistent, and yet at the same time so powerful that it cannot be completely ignored despite all attempts not to follow it. Everyone is looking for their being. Everyone is looking for love.

Being, love, and truth: this is your Holy Trinity, the perpetual reality of your existence, your divine creation, unique and unrepeatable.

19.

Ecstasy of a Heart in Love

Words heard by a soul who has chosen only love, having been infused with the living Christ within

I. Introduction

(From Sebastián)

During this session, Mother Mary told me that she was aware of the feeling of my soul, and of her joy for my having returned to her being, that is, to the Divine Love she is. When she said that, a vision of the living Christ who lives in me became present in all its glory. It was the glory of the Father, the beauty of love, and the magnificence of souls—all of them, in their essence. Unlike all other manifestations in which the message arrived instantaneously as symbols and music that were interpreted by Archangel Raphael, I directly saw images that were able to be humanly described, and I also heard the words below.

II. In Praise of Love

Oh, holy love! Divine Love! You created everything that exists, moves, and is. You are the essence of life. Your strength is more powerful than the energy of the universe, your softness more beautiful than the tenderness of a spring breeze, your scent sweeter than the nectar of a flower. Who invokes you is sated in your beauty. Who looks for you, finds you.

Oh, purity of Divine Love! Poets can but seek metaphors with which to approach your beauty. Who can hold you down? Who can silence your sweet voice? Wherever I look I find you, for you are everywhere.

Holy infinite love, essence of my being and of all life, in the dark of night I found you. There you were illuminous, present with the tenderness of your heart, like the dim moonlight. By day I saw you in all your brilliance. I recognized you in the sweetness of your unmistakable voice. Your presence is for me what the wind is for the birds as they undertake flight. You are rest, you are movement, you are the game of beautiful love. Without you nothing would exist. In you everything rejoices in the joy of living.

The birds sing. The leaves that fell from the tree that gave them life are now lifted by the wind as if your arms raised them to take them to Heaven as an expression of your benevolence.

Every morning the nightingale sings to you. Flowers bless you every night when you go to sleep. Every drop of water sighs for you, plunging into the depths of rivers, seas, and oceans, like the souls that seek you merge with you.

Oh, miracle of life, extension of truth, pure expression of perfect love! Marigolds are born from your belly, and from your mind the noblest desires. From your heart arise the most beautiful melodies, from your eyes come rays of light that illuminate the entire universe.

Oh, holy love, love of gratitude, love without opposite! You are the delight of the wise and the sleeplessness of lovers. No one can cage you. You can never be held by one hand, yet in every friendly hand you exist.

Oh, force of love that puts a smile on the faces of hearts in love and calms the storms of minds stunned by the noisy world!

Oh, peace, you live in love! You are one with me, because I am one with love.

Oh, sweetness of divine perfection, purity of a love without beginning or end or width in creation, longing for those who seek the truth! You have been scribed by those who, unable to remain silent, write to make you known to the world. For you songs have been sung, paintings portrayed, and sculptures formed, giving life to marble or gold.

Oh, mystery of beautiful love, living miracle of a power unseen but felt, a force unheard but which manifests!

Oh, holy Divine Love, sweetness of angels and ecstasy of lovers! You surround me everywhere, there where my feet fall and where my eyes look.

Time will pass and you will continue to create life. The planets will pass, the lives of humanity will pass, sunrises and sunsets will pass, but you will always be new, always loving, always creating life.

Where do the sunrises go? Where does the night go when day comes? They go to nothing, they come back to you, the love that creates life, love without borders, love without condition.

Where do bodies go when they are no longer in the world? To you, my beloved. They return to you, the breath of life, the vital force that calls matter into existence. What moves, moves in you. What sings, sings in you. What sighs, sighs in you. What suffers, suffers in you. What screams, screams at you. You are the source of life. Creative love. Holy love. Perfect love. Essence of being. Love that creates life. Love in fullness. You who give life to the trees, their branches, their leaves, to the grass, the Earth and the sky. You who created my soul to be yours. You are the joy of my existence. You are what my being has been looking for, forever. You are the reason for my existence, the shelter of my mind, the joy of my heart in love.

In silence, I find you. In noise, I long for you. In peace I rejoice in you. In the storm, I look for you. In light I see you reflected in all your glory. In the night, I invoke you and you come. Every beat of my heart belongs to you, for you are the reason of my life and the love of my loves. A love that creates life. Love of holiness. Love in whose light I love. Origin of life and purpose of existence.

Oh holy love! Extend your arms to me. Let us stay together, embraced in an ecstasy of love. One day, crying, I called you. Another day, happy, I found you. I sang songs for having come back to life. My heart vibrates upon hearing your voice. My mind rests in peace upon knowing your truth.

Oh, holy love, in whom I have merged for all eternity! You and I are one, like waters of the same river.

Oh, joy of the heart that lives in love with God, who always lives happily in the certainty of being loved, who sings a song to life in communion with the beloved.

Oh, blissful soul in love! By singing to the beat of the Sacred Heart, becoming one with life, plunging into the infinite ocean of love, your consciousness of being, you come back to life. You return to love, to the Mother's house, where you have never really been absent.

Oh, bliss of the loving heart, lover of God, You live always in safety even in the midst of storms, remaining serene and peaceful. You are like a tree planted from the seed of truth that the winds cannot move. Nothing can rip you from the arms of your beloved.

Oh, foundation of holy love, foundation of life, creation rests on you. You are firmer than the firmest rock. You are sweeter than honey.

Joy of a soul in love! God is your contentment, creator, and eternal companion in love. In God you live happily every day of your life. In God you live united to love.

Oh, face of holy love, how beautiful you are! Your gaze melts hearts hardened by the heartbreak of the world. Immerse them in the beauty of your divinity.

This sacred one in the heart of love fears nothing, because he lives with his beloved. Nothing bothers him, because he knows his beloved. Nothing confuses him, because he knows he is loved.

Oh, holy love, shelter of minds that seek the truth, strength of those who seek God! I long for that soul, the realization of the angels, perfection of the universe, diversity in creation. Everything that exists, exists for you and in you. You gave us life, so that we know you; and knowing you, we are forever happy in the grace of beautiful love, in the purity of Divine Love, in the greatness of your holiness.

Oh, pure love, food for the soul! You are the blessing of lovers and loved ones, joy to the heart that lives together with its God.

Oh, beloved Christ! You are the love in which everything was made. You are the love of life, the joy of my heart, the love to which my soul sings, the love that my heart seeks, the life that my being wants to live, the truth that the mind with so much effort has sought to find.

Oh, my beloved Christ! Love of my loves, joy of my heart, refuge of my mind, in you I rejoice for all eternity.

Oh, my beloved Christ who became one with me! I am all yours. My thoughts belong to you. My feelings are for you.

My beloved Christ of incomparable beauty, infinite goodness, and endless mercy, you are the hope of the world. You are what creation is waiting for. You are the home we are going to. You are the Heaven in which we already live. Our consciousness rests joyfully in you. Our memory wants to remember only you. Our understanding seeks to understand the mysteries of Heaven, because in them it finds you.

Oh, my beloved Christ! I reveal my soul. I give myself to you. You are my everything. My soul was thirsty for you, but you have calmed her. You have given her drink from the waters of eternal life.

III. The Response of the Beloved

Beloved soul, you came out of My being. You are the delight of My heart, living miracle of my divinity, always conceived to be the vessel of My wisdom and recipient of My holy love. Let us together tell the world about the sweetness of our union, the purity of our beautiful love. Now that the journey in which you searched for Me is over, we will let the light of our divine relationship be seen by all who seek the truth, because they seek love. Sensitive hearts, those most called to love, will recognize in our words and deeds the voice and the movement of truth they long for, since their hearts know what My being is. They live in us, just as we live in them.

Hearts that find the love that unites us, you, and all those who are of the truth, live happily in the realization of their being. Their souls sing happy songs. Their minds tell happy stories. Through the purity of their vision, they see the love they are. They are resurrected to the sanctity of being. They are the ones who have returned to love.

When the soul meets love, everything changes within. The days are brighter, the nights are no longer dark, the beauty of the stars and the moon can be seen. Shadows are no longer feared, since once the heart is happy in the eternal meeting with the beloved, they simply represent one more way to reflect the soul. The mind plays with them, having fun with their forms. Thus, the days are a blessed scenario where shadows give knowledge of what is happening in the mind's projections. Never again are they feared.

Now the shadows are what they are: one more way to know. There is no reason to cancel them. You watch them and let them be. They are allowed to come when they come. The mind recognizes that this occurs when the sun is behind it. You observe that and say: "Oh, I have turned around. I am turning my back to the light." And then you do the only thing necessary, turn your eyes to the sun, contemplating the light of the beloved face to face again, continuing to receive the warmth of that embrace and continuing forever to feel the ecstasy of the beauty of that light.

For the soul in love, there is only the sleeplessness of living together with Her love. If you look closely at this statement of truth, you will see the perfect certainty that resides in it. With this I want to tell you, My beloved, that for the heart that has found Me there is only one sigh. Your mind is fixed on love. Your soul focuses on love. Your being lives submerged in love. Your body reflects the love in which memory, understanding, and will remain tied together like a bouquet of beautiful flowers.

Only love can gather together everything that is part of your being, because those scattered parts that were previously bewildered, had their origin in it. In order to live in harmony, it is necessary to love and let yourself be loved. Receive and give constantly. When you decide to live that way, all your movements become loving again regardless of how they manifest themselves, for they are all love. In that state, which is the state of reunion, your memory brings memories of love, your imagination imagines ways to love, your intelligence discerns what love is and unravels its infinity, the heart feels the joy of loving and being loved, the will prepares to be alone with the Beloved. Herein lies joy.

The soul in love does not concern itself much with the affairs of the world, except for the opportunity it offers to receive and give love. She lives without worrying too much about herself. He forgets himself. He does not even care much about feeding or dressing well, much less being distracted from his contemplation. She is consumed in love. He is one with his beloved divine, with thoughts only for love. Your whole being rejoices.

IV. The Response to Union

When the soul is united—or more accurately, when it meets its essence—it cannot love anything other than what it is because nothing outside itself has value. For love, unreality does not exist. Just as the heart knows what love is, so your soul knows what Christ is. The knowledge of being is perfect. Nothing confuses it. It enjoys truth. This gift received by the soul simply is what it is, and cannot be eliminated or lost.

Hearts that respond to love welcome your unity not only with love but with each other. There is no distance between one soul in love and another. Lovers recognize love. This recognition by the being of love is inherent. You can easily recognize this capacity by observing creation. Peers know that they are peers. This knowledge is innate and cannot be acquired or lost. It is what leads birds of a feather to fly together.

The mind returned to truth is not only capable of recognizing what one has become, but is attracted to it. It, in turn, is attracted to what is similar to it. In unity, the mind acts like a magnet; all truth joins it, like iron filings to the magnetic force of love.

Once the heart is free to love what it desires to love, it cannot love anything else. The high only joins with what is in the heights.

At this point in the spiritual path, it is important to remember that the essence of your being is like the water of a stream which rises to the sky to satisfy its desire to be rain. When it ascends it does so to irrigate the land that needs to be watered. Where had that water that was in the creek come from but the rain? This is the cycle of life. This is the cycle of love.

Love comes from Heaven. In it resides its source. It is not of the world, although it may be in it. Love is divine. How divine is your being!

If the waters of Heaven descend to fulfill their mission and then return, why would you think you do not do the same?

Very literally you are a droplet that has descended to Earth as a blessed emanation of the being of pure love that God is. Once you have watered the soil from which life is born, you will return from whence you came. You will not continue to be the water of eternal life, but will be the light that shines everywhere. You return to the sun.

While life is not energy in the same sense as electrical or mechanical energy, it is similar. Everything that exists is coated with energy—vital energy in the sense of strength or power.

Just as energy is transformed, so is the soul force, or spiritual energy, that constitutes your being. It is accurate to compare your soul to a droplet that, once raised, becomes light. The energy that transforms the droplet is the same energy that gives life to the sun. In other words, the essence of energy is the same in every manifestation of it, regardless of the form it takes. The same goes for each being: all are born of the same substance and are made up of it. Each one adopts its form according to the will that created it.

Every body, every thought, every beat of every heart, every flow of every drop of blood, every breeze and every living being, every feeling felt, is a form that being adopts. All come from love, because love is the source of existence.

If love is the essence of being and that from which all life arises, when the heart meets with love you are meeting with your Source. We call this returning the return to truth. Once it has met what it is, the soul cannot do anything other than that for which it was created: spread love and enjoy love.

It is of great importance that we restore in your memory the direct association that exists between bliss and love. This is because often in a bleak past that has nothing to do with truth, love has been linked to suffering. Loving and being loved is the joy of the heart that lives for love. It is the joy of the soul that has returned to the arms of the divine Beloved. It is the fullness of being because it was not created for anything else.

To enjoy eternally My presence is the gift that I have always given you as a creation, since in Me everything is endless joy. In love there is no room for sadness. In love there is only the light that gives life to everything that joins. Undoubtedly it can embrace misery, just as truth can embrace illusion and reason can embrace madness, but whenever it does, it ends up transmuting them into more love.

V. The Joy of Truth

It has been said that everything is consciousness. Therefore if that statement be true, love must also be consciousness. We shall discuss this now.

Love, being the substance of all substances, is the source of consciousness. In fact, the creation of consciousness is an act of God's love. The Creator, with perfect wisdom, created your being and endowed you with the ability to know yourself, because that is how God can know the holiness, harmony, and other treasures of the Kingdom. In doing so the being participates in divine jubilation, which consists of ecstasy in the contemplation of its beauty, from which all goodness, all life, and all holiness arises.

There is no greater joy for the being than knowing oneself in the truth that has been created, and extending that knowledge eternally. This is the only definition of joy that makes sense to you who, having received these words, receive love forever in your heart and truth in your holy mind.

Since truth is love made right, and as such it is the cause of life, there is nothing for which the soul can truly yearn other than the holiness in which she is truth. This is why a mind that has been healed and has returned to innocence only wants to be what it is, just as God created it. It no longer fears truth or love.

Now you know that truth is the cause of your freedom and also your beloved companion. You will never be separate from truth because having heard and followed its voice you have recognized your holiness. In your full innocence you have rejoined the beauty of what you are. Sister, you no longer fear yourself. Brother, you know, since you have seen and heard it in your heart, that there is no reason for anything but the joy of living. She has returned to life and recognized her unchanging innocence. He has forgiven himself and forgiven everyone.

Like flowers blooming in springtime, so the soul reunited with its divine Beloved opens to receive an endless flow of holy love. The small stream in the desert is overflowing, growing and growing until it floods and gives new life where there was barren land.

Sing with joy, soul who has returned to love! Dying to the world, your feet no longer touch the ground, your arms extend to the sky. Her open hands are an incessant plea, asking God to fill her eternally with more love. Her eyes only look at the beloved. Her breathing becomes one with her divine Beloved, because now His love is the air she breathes and the food that gives her life.

The mind that has stripped itself of illusions to give way to the truth needs nothing. In it shines the sun of wisdom. In its abode dwells holiness. In its thoughts there is only God and everything that refers to Him. It lives safely in the certainty of holiness. It has met the one who lives within. It knows and is glad in knowing the mirror where Christ is reflected, where the light of truth lives so it can enlighten the world. Know who speaks to your heart. Vividly remember the love of your loves. Live thinking only of God.

The attention of the heart is fixed on the object of love, on God, because when love makes an appearance, the consciousness of love awakens in truth. Now you do not cease living in love.

What can a mind lack whose only need is to live in the truth, once it has recognized that it, itself, is the eternal truth since it is one with the divine mind? And what can a heart that lives in love need once it understands that the love it so much longs for is itself, having been made one with the Sacred Heart?

Nothing is missing from the soul that lives in the fullness of love. Nothing is lacking who lives in God.

20.

Bliss and Being

A message in the Voice of Mother-Father God, the Voice of All Voices

I. Prelude

Oh, My soul, born of My being and gathered in My love, soul that belongs to Me from all eternity! How much joy it is to be here, reunited with you!

I am your Mother and Creator. I am the love you have sought. I am the truth that has found you and the holiness you are and in which you live. Your return is a light to the world and an extension of creation. Your union with Me is the great banquet table of salvation, the most sacred gift conceivable.

Living together with you is joy for My divinity and joy for your heart of love. And it is a song for your holy mind.

How much bliss is in Heaven and on Earth because of these dialogues of love! We are reaching the end of the sixth book of this work of love and kindness. You are becoming increasingly aware of the divine relationship that exists between you and Me.

I love you. You love Me. And in our love we gather everyone equally. No one is excluded from the benevolence that flows from our relationship. Everything is embraced by our union of holiness.

The true strength of our love goes beyond anything that can be understood, because our union is the source of being. It is what has given life to everything.

Because of the time you spent with Me receiving these words, countless miracles have happened and will continue to happen. They will be miracles of resurrection. Many hearts will begin to sing again. Many minds will remember the truth of what they are and will rejoice in what they will see. All this and much more is emerging in creation as an effect of your willingness to unite in spirit and truth through this work that I give you for love.

A divine relationship is powerful. Within it are the mysteries of Heaven and all life takes on the vital force it needs to keep itself always new, always loved, always holy. There is no sincere love that is not a source of miracles and life because love is the source of miracles and life. There is no other source. There is no other reality than love.

What a joy it is to dwell with you. My heart joins yours in an ecstasy of purity and light. We are one reality. We are one holy love. In the light of My glory I called you. From the light of My holiness I extended the rays of My being to embrace your soul. Nothing and no one can ever separate us. We are the meeting place of love, the sacred mountain, the sweetness of truth, the twinkle of wisdom that emanates strength to enlightened minds.

Sing, soul in love! Dance, pure heart! Scrutinize, mind, that you have returned to truth. Vibrate, emanate from the light. You have penetrated the mystery of mysteries. You have met Me. And with that, you have met My Heart, which is unknown to anyone who does not choose to live in love. Together we have raised the fallen love, bringing it back to the top of the celestial mountain in which we will live together forever. From there we have extended it to Heaven, making what belonged to Me return to the blessed abodes of My heart.

Come all! Come, enjoy the delights of Divine Love, a love that is a blessing to lovers and the delight of loved ones. Do not deprive yourself of the graces of My Sacred Heart, divine children who are sprouts of My eternal Motherhood. Sing a new song, the song of beautiful love. Live joyfully in me. In our union you will see things you have not even imagined in holiness and beauty.

Within our union I have transformed you into the divinity that you have always been, although one day you wanted to believe—although not with all your will—to be what I never wanted you to be.

Oh, beloved child! Vibrant heart! Purity of a love like no other! No love in the world can resemble the love of the divine lover and his Beloved. No one can love you as I can. In the same way, you cannot love anyone as you love Me, because I am the love in which you love. It is from our divine relationship, a unique relationship full of the love of holiness, from where your heart is nourished to love all things. The heart that finds Me changes. The soul who has fallen in love with this divine lover who is your Mother and Creator jumps for joy.

Who can take care of you as I do? Who can watch over you as your eternal Lover does? No one. Because there is nothing and no one who knows you like Me and can know what your heart plots as a loving and loved child.

The words of love and truth flow in the mind that lives in spirit without form. Thoughts of light shine majestically in the mind that has returned to life.

I am the nameless one in which every name exists. I am the faceless being, from whom every face is born. I am the sweetness of love. I am the beauty from which all beauty emanates. United in our being, as one mind, one holy heart, one truth, we are the unity of being.

What a joy to remain by your side and in you. All My love envelops you in the solace of Heaven that I am. Remember, My child, that these words are full of life. They are for you who have decided, for the love of holiness, to dedicate some time to being alone with your Mother. Your presence and My essence have become one in our meeting.

How much joy it is for the Mother to be able to receive Her sons and daughters and be graced with Her company.

Absorb yourself in My light. Consume yourself in My being. Immerse yourself in My divinity. Come, drink from the water of life. I am the nectar of Heaven come down in the way you occupy body and mind. You are the Christ on Earth. You are the presence of My love in the world. Every day you will love with more love, until the strength of your heart shakes the foundations upon which the illusion of the world stands. And together we will gather multitudes of sisters and brothers to take them by the hand to the holy meeting.

II. Harmony and Reality

We are coming to an end. Each time one of these holy books which make up this work ends, a new beginning starts. A renewal occurs in your soul. At each end, a beginning. Each time its end. Happy are they who can understand this sweet truth.

Truly, truly I tell you that I will never leave you and you will never leave Me without the joy of your beauty. Oh, holy soul, pure and perfect, how much joy it is to have you in My arms! What peace Heaven feels when we know that in our union we will remain forever immersed in the love that creates life in abundance, love in fullness. Let yourself be flooded by love. Let yourself be filled with holiness. Let the force that flows from My loving heart reach the center of your being and from there impregnate your mind, your reality, and the entire world.

Children from all over the world, do not deny the beauty of Divine Love. Do not deprive yourself of My delights, or turn away from the sky that dwells in your hearts. Each of you is a glass into which you can pour the essence of My being. Your consciousness can know me, just as this helping hand writing from Heaven and lover of his Creator, is helping you to recognize.

These words are your words. They were born in the depths of your being. They are written for your soul. They are words that your divinized humanity sings. In them your heart recognizes the voice of the Beloved, whom you now remember vividly and will soon fully recognize yourself as your being. This work is not external to you. It is part of your holy reality. You have joined it. When you dedicate to travel with it, you attain a greater degree of consciousness of what is beyond your mind, yet is as much yours as your soul is.

Each fiber of your being is embedded in the flow that exists between this work and you, because when you enter these dialogues, you enter the flow of union. Something inside you shudders sweetly upon hearing My voice.

To live in this divine relationship is to live in love. To remain in the presence of your being is to be aware of who you are. Herein lies the fact of returning to truth. Although there is still a small section to be traveled in the world, a limited reality in terms of the ability to be aware of the totality and extend that awareness to everyone and everything, nevertheless in this reality we can together begin to live our Heaven of perfect love.

If you focus your life on what you have to do for God, you will fall into the error of trying to live from the truth in the terms of Heaven when you are still treading Earth with a unique consciousness that has not yet reached complete detachment from partial vision. Remember, this is the world of perception. Nothing in it is true. It cannot be, because perceiving and knowing are not the same. Remember also not to confuse what is the same with what is different.

Many have been lost on the road because of wanting to bring Heaven to Earth in a way contrary to the truth, that is, to love. You are called to do so without losing sight of the reality in which you live forever in Jesus and Mary.

Before finalizing this sixth book and entering the end of the work in which we walk the path of being, it is of great importance to understand what it means to create a new Heaven and a new Earth, or in other words, to bring Heaven to Earth. We will speak to that. Both expressions try to express the same thing, creating a state of consciousness or reality based on love. There is no other Heaven than truth. There is no other Kingdom of Heaven than love.

III. Happiness and Awareness

The risk into which you could fall, and that would make you temporarily lose time and joy, is to believe you must do something with what you are given in this revelation or that you must take the action of sharing with others what you have received, believing that the goal is to transform the world or yourself. The world and you are one. The world lives in your mind, not outside of who you are. There are only your thoughts and their union with your feelings. The rest is pure mental gymnastics and has nothing to do with reality.

As you already know, there is nothing outside of you. That includes both Heaven and the world. So all you have to do is be the love you really are. Neither Jesus nor Mary ever set a goal of doing anything in particular. They were everything. Ultimately that is the goal, if it can be called such, for you and for everyone who wants to live in harmony with what they are in Truth.

The goal we promulgate here is to be happy. There is not, nor can there be, another purpose for the spiritual path if it brings you to the being that you truly are. You were created to be happy. Happiness is not simply a wish, it is the reality of your being. So to create a new Heaven and a new Earth, or bring Heaven to Earth, is to constantly reflect happiness. Of course, this happiness, and as we have said, has nothing to do with the limited idea of worldly happiness, which is always elusive and passing.

Lasting, eternal happiness is what is spoken of here. You must now extend the bliss of being who you are. You know what I am referring to because the wisdom of your being knows happiness. In fact, regardless of whether you sought happiness in illusions or in the truth, if you have been able to conceive of the idea of happiness it is only because you know it exists.

What does not bring lasting happiness has no place in your mind or your heart. Observance is still necessary; be alert to anything that happens inside you that denotes unhappiness. Of course, no one consciously wishes to be unhappy. This is a universal understanding. Unhappiness is unconsciousness. The pursuit of happiness is the search for being, which in turn is the search for love. With this truth shining in your holy mind, you will recognize that happiness is inherent in the being that God created you to be as always conceived.

Being truly yourself and being happy are the same. You are not only love, you are truth and happiness. It follows that radiating joy, telling happy stories, having loving thoughts, and not harboring or spreading what hurts the heart, is the path of correct discernment in the light of truth. Those who choose love above all else are the realized ones. They may or may not satisfy their material or psychological needs. They do not consider doing so essential. Those who live in love can say authentically with Mary: "All generations will call me happy."

Mary is an example of perfect happiness, an exemplary life for you who have been graced with the gift of these words. You are invited to travel the path of Mary. It is a way of being, a path of incarnation and creation. It is a way of giving birth to Christ, delivering the love of God, of harboring feelings of compassion toward everyone. Mary's path has no intention of changing anything. It recognizes that love is a silent presence, full of light and holiness.

The silence of Mary must become an example for your life. In her you can find the mystery of the incarnation and salvation. Mary received everything from God. To Him she consecrated her existence. In her there is no shadow of separation, because she lives with her eyes fixed on her Divine Beloved, the light of her being. She accepts everything with love and sweetness, because she knows that everything comes from love. She does not confuse what is love with what is not. Mary always remains in the truth.

Is it possible to live in truth while in the world? Yes. Therefore, living in the happiness of being is possible too. The being that God has always arranged for you to be is a being of pure truth. To be the love you are, you simply have to live in the truth that you know very well. You know what is true, everyone knows it. You know what love is, everyone knows it. You also know what makes you good, what makes you happy, what gives you peace and joy. You know how to smile with your heart.

Since you were created with the knowledge of love, truth, and happiness, the purpose of your creation can only be to be happy in the love you are. Since the love you really are is the same love that God is—and is no other love than God's—then it follows that you were created to be happy in God's love.

How simple is the truth! We travelled the winding roads of the world to find something we could not put into words, but our hearts knew it very well. That "I don't know what," which worries the human heart and even leads it to commit crazy things, is none other than a creative force united to the desire for endless happiness.

How notable that such a clear and simple purpose, so universal and so inherent in the hearts of women and men of all time and places, has been so neglected or transformed into what can never be. Why? Although this question has already been answered in many ways in these writings of love and truth, we can delve further into it.

Obviously, everyone wants to be happy. But what does this actually mean? For some it is one thing, for others it is another, and because they differentiate among themselves as to what it takes to make each one happy, they remain in conflict, not only between sisters and brothers, but between humanity and God. God's idea of what happiness is, is the only real definition, just as with truth and love.

What we are doing here is to unite the consciousness of the reality of being with truth. The being you are is eternally happy. Christ does not change, but lives in endless bliss, because Christ is the source of joy, the source of being. To return to love is to return to being. By remaining aware of the being you really are, you are happy. Being love remains the only option, because being anything else is attempting to be what you are not.

Nothing outside the joy of being exists, or exists outside of love. Thus the experience of misery is a temporary one that, like everything in the world of dual consciousness, enables the contrast of opposites. Remember that comparing opposites is how the separated mind tries to understand.

Happiness is Christ. This is because Christ is the being God created you to be, you along with everything that exists. To make this truth how you live in the world is to bring Heaven to Earth.

You may be wondering why we touch this issue now, as we have already talked about it from different perspectives. The reason is because I do not want you to fall into the error of believing that creating a new Heaven and a new Earth is a task to be performed, or one that involves eliminating the current world and replacing it with another. There is nothing wrong with the world as it is. It is the perfect reality where you can return to love through your ability to choose. The experience you have here on this plane allows you to do it very well. There is no reason why you should not live in direct relationship with God while you are in the world. You are beautiful, and the world is, too. You are holy, as is the world. Remember that everything that joins Me is made holy because of who I am, just as with what joins you.

If My holiness joins the world with you, why should we continue to fear it or consider it unworthy?

When you gather everything and everyone into your heart, you make Heaven and Earth come together in you. Then you can say: your kingdom has come, your will is done.

To include everyone in the embrace of love is to create a new Heaven and a new Earth. To keep everyone within the being that you really are, and keep them in your heart as if this were the universe where they live protected by love, is to create a refuge where hearts can live in peace, that is, bringing Heaven to the world, for it is true: we are one heart.

21.

The Gift of Divine Relationship

A message in the Voice of Father-Mother God, the Voice of All Voices

I. Prelude

My beloved, once again I come to dwell with you and be the comfort of your soul, the joy of your heart, and the refuge of your holy mind. Fear not. Have no worries. I am your Father, Mother, and Creator. I love you and I take care of you. My joy is the happiness of My children. My joy is to see you smile every day of your life, starting now and continuing forever.

Beloved son, beloved daughter, joy of a God of pure love, miracle that emerged from My Sacred Heart, there is no heart in this world that has not cried. Let that show you that the human heart knows what eternal bliss is. It knows what love is.

You who have returned to your heart will now find it to be a perfect guide to the Heaven of your being. Rejoice, you have returned to truth! You have found the way, the truth, and the life, and will never lose your way again. Not only are you endless bliss and perfect love, you are the resurrection and eternal life because you are created of My divinity.

From all eternity I chose you for this work which is accomplished in your soul through the reception of these words. There is only one relevant thing in existence: love. The rest has no space in the universe of My divinity because there is no such thing as "the rest." Only love is real. Only love is strong. Only love is eternal.

Now that you are aware of your deliberate decision made out of time, in union with My being, to return home, we will be blessing the world before leaving for the abode of the wise, to the house of formless truth.

The world needs your blessing as much as you need the air you breathe because we are one soul, one divine mind, united in the reality of love. Without our joint blessing, love could not exist in the world, and that would make it a real hell until it ceased to exist completely for lack of love. Remember that those without love faint. The same applies to all creation.

We have been united in this particular way, in this work, this gift of My love to My beloved daughters and sons. This way of uniting is sacred, and there is no other like it; it is unique. We are two gathered in the unity of being, meaning that what was separated has come together as one flesh, one heart, one reality—you and I, united in pure holy love. There is no longer a distance between your being and My being. There is no son or daughter and Father as separate entities that relate to each other; there is now only our union, a union that will gradually shine in all its glory and illuminate the world.

To you who for love of Me have dedicated this time to receive and share My word—the voice of the heart that lives in you—I tell you that you have been transformed such that no trace remains of your old reality. That old person will never come back. What joy it is to be born again! What joy is the certainty of knowing who you are! The joy of knowing your true being.

Now I ask you to be willing to abandon the path we have been traveling together, to leave all behind and not to long for it, to open yourself to a new reality based on our relationship of pure eternal love, as the sign of the joy of being who you really are.

Noon is nigh. The sun shines in all its magnificence. Light embraces everything. Let the universe be happy. A holy being has been recognized and therefore loved. A new star will shine in the firmament of eternal life, a star that has your name and will shine with the beauty of who you are.

Beloved of this God of pure love who undoes everything in union with you! Realize how much I as your Father am willing to do to attract you to My Divine Love. I have inspired this helping hand, have moved the heart of this soul in love, and have taken his time to let everyone know the wonders of My love. In My Sacred Heart lies Heaven. In My love lives your endless bliss. I am the joy without opposite speaking directly to you who are the light of My eyes, the beauty, the miracle of love and truth.

Our love makes us both great because now we are one; and in our unity infinite greatness is expressed in all its reality. There is no place where you are not because the universe is the abode of My heart. In it resides the water of life, the wind of the spirit, and the light of wisdom that illuminates every human. I am the living word. I am the eternal reality of love.

We have reached a point where we are able to enjoy the beauty of your heart, making you aware of its throb. This takes you directly into My arms, and in them you will remain forever, united to the source of endless life.

II. Our Union Is Eternal

The world will pass, planets will pass, oceans and mountains will pass, everything of the world will pass. But our love will never pass. Truly, truly I tell you that everything from the book of time will in due time be erased, but you will never pass because your name is written in the book of life.

Child of My heart, now I wish to speak to the whole world through your hands and your intelligence, together with your love, for you are a vessel of wisdom, an instrument of love, a channel of grace that has no opposite.

Understand that all of what is said here resonates in all hearts in unison. It is not said for one, but for all the children of My being. Each one of you is My helping hand, the glass where the wisdom of My divinity is poured. What your heart feels and your mind thinks is like the wind. You know not from where it comes or where it goes. Your spirit blows always with the reality of life. It is on the move like unfathomable oceans, full of inner life. You are light that embellishes everything it touches. You are a living miracle. You are saints because you are Mine.

I tell you with love and truth: cease looking, for you have found. Do not follow teachers. You do not need them, for your inner teacher—your heart united to your mind—will henceforth and forever be the perfect guide to the fullness of being. Let go of everything you learned. Let it go calmly, for a time of calm and love is coming, a time of joy and ease. You will receive a hundred for one. My love will never leave you.

This work is manifested because you need My love, although many believe not. The universe cannot continue to live without receiving the flow of love, an extension of Myself, that emanates from My being. Although others believe they can disregard the love I am, you know it is not true. You know because you have heard the voice of your heart and followed it. You have chosen only love as your eternal choice.

Do not refuse eternal life. Always remain in My love. You know it well. Waste no time on complex studies; they only create confusion and fear. There is only one reality, love. There is only one real choice, love. There is only one true path, love.

Your life has changed much since we started this path. The changes may not be visible yet, but will soon be. You are not what one day you were. Today, here, now and forever, you can be reborn in love if you so dispose. There is no reason to stagnate in old structures, or to continue thinking that the life you have had so far has to remain the same. Life is always new. Love is eternal novelty.

I am by your side every day. If you want to keep Me away in your consciousness, you can do so. That will not cause My love to diminish, although you will deprive yourself of the joy of our union of divine spouses, a union of heart to heart, a unity that makes the union of the divine and the human extend forever.

You can't help Me love you. You cannot cause it to go where you go. I always care for you as a mother cares for her offspring. Know well that these are not simply words that cause the heart to rejoice and the soul to vibrate to the beat of My divinity; they are true words, full of life and love.

If I have created you with the possibility of choice, it is because I also created everything necessary for you to live in love and receive all you need, in all times, places, and circumstances. I do not ignore My creations. They are the reason for My creative being.

You who receive this gift from Heaven, My word of eternal life expressed in this way, know that I love you with perfect love, that you are in all My thoughts, that every beat of My heart has an echo in yours. We are an eternal unity and will be forever united in truth. Everything your heart longed for is here in our divine relationship. In it you will find the strength to live, the wisdom to discern, and the joy to play the game of life without worry, tension or tiredness.

I give you our direct relationship. It is a gift and a grace. It is a treasure without equal. I give it to you because of your love for Me and My love for you. Everyone can access this treasure of grace, establishing a conscious relationship of pure love with Me. My will is to live together in an eternal relationship in which everything that My being is, is given to all. It depends on each one to accept My gift or not. You are free, always free.

The world may not understand Me, or may not understand the greatness of this gift from Heaven, to be able to live forever united to My perfect love. But that does not change My will, for I am immutable. My love never changes. Truly, I am eternal wisdom.

You who believe in all kinds of miracles, or at least a great variety of them, do you recognize this as the miracle of miracles? A wonder that surpasses every measure and knowledge of the world?

Even you who do not believe in miracles believe in many impossible things, such as that you can live without love. Realize who is speaking to you, and with how much grace I speak from eternity without form, making of Me a human word, a symbol of love and forgiveness for a world that needs peace.

Listen. Among the trees, I am the tree of life. Among creators, I am the creator of love. Everything that exists finds its beginning in Me. Among all knowledge, I am the knowledge of the soul. Among all wisdom, I am the wisdom of love. Among many paths, I am the only one that leads to truth. I am eternal time. I am the creator of life who sees all, the eye that sees into every corner of the universe. Nothing escapes My benevolence. Everything is wrapped in My being. Of all sounds, I am the first. I am the force that moves the seas. All light goes to Me and emanates from Me. I am kindness in those who are good, and beauty where there is beauty. I am the silence where sacred mysteries hide. I am the knowledge of those who truly know.

I am the seed of everything. Without Me there would be nothing that moves and nothing that remains motionless. My divine greatness is without end. The words of this work reveal but a tiny part of My infinite glory, My unfathomable love for you. Just know that everything that is beautiful or good, every spark of glory or power that you appreciate, is part of My nature. I maintain the entire universe. Truly, I Am.

Those who offer Me their love obtain the grace of seeing Me through spiritual vision and remain within our divine relationship. Only for love can you receive My knowledge. I reveal Myself to all who come to Me with humility and love in their hearts, sincerely wishing to know the truth. You who love Me and for whom I am your supreme goal, already freed from illusions, and with immense love for all that exists, you, indeed, come to Me.

I do not tell you these things, beloved child, to overwhelm you with the divinity of My being. Nothing and no one can ever define Me, and you cannot count the days of My life. I am the unfathomable immensity of being. All forms are born in Me. All energies arise from Me. Everything is Mine, for I am the sovereign of the universe. Truly, I am love.

I tell you these things which you know very well so that you remember who you are. You cannot continue to believe in a God as big as the universe, and in a child as small as a grain of sand. Now the child has merged into Mother-Father God. The water droplet has become an ocean of life. Love has merged with love to create a new love.

III. Come All

Love and I are one. This will be from now and forever the truth of your reality. Not because now it is and before was not, but because now it will be the truth that governs your days. God has come to Earth in you. Christ has been reborn in the beauty of your heart. A holy love was born from our relationship, the fruit of My divinity and your humanity, divinized human, love that gives life, creative love.

In our relationship of unity lies everything that has given life to all that exists. I am no longer the one who cannot be known, or whose infinite heart remains a mystery. Now that you have recognized love, there is no reason that everything that I am is not familiar to you. Just as a mother does not set limits on her love for her child, in the same way there are no limits between you and Me.

Our relationship is established. We have created a new portal in which the direct relationship with God flows without interruption from the reality of love to the world and everything in it. No aspect of creation is untouched by our relationship. This beautiful love story, which is what our union is about, is balm for the thirsty hearts of love, joy for the birds of the sky, and inspiration for many human minds.

Children of all times and corners of the world! Remember every word in this work, not with your thinking minds or with your cognitive memories, but in your heart, the abode of Christ. You have felt many things along this path we have traveled together. Treasure those feelings. Love them. They are the living expression of our relationship.

You will not feel alone any more, or helpless, or at the mercy of a world that plucks you from here to there like a blowing autumn leaf. No, for now you have full right to say about yourself:

"My Mother-Father and I are one, therefore I am also the Tree of Life. I am the wind that blows in spirit, giving life to everything that lives. I am love spreading throughout eternity. I am one with God. I am the manifested power of the Mother-Father's love. I am the alpha and the omega because my Mother-Father is."

Everything of the parent belongs to the child. These words are visible manifestation of the child's inheritance. What other inheritance could a child of love receive except a divine relationship?

Our relationship can achieve anything because there is nothing that holiness cannot achieve in our union of divine spouses, merged into one body, one soul, one reality, where you are as I created you to be. There you return to the happiness of the soul. In our union you are aware of the love that created you because it is there you receive it without interruption.

How our relationship is manifested is everyone's business. It will never be the same, because we are life. We are movement. We are the vibrant force of love. The only important thing to know about our union is that it is an indissoluble union of pure Divine Love. This is not something that can be known with the thinking mind, with the intellectual thought system. It simply is what it is: the direct relationship between Creator and created.

It is impossible to put limits on our relationship, because it is always new. Remember that in every moment you die and are reborn in My glory. In every moment, the world and humans are renewed without being aware of their constant change. Life is eternal novelty. Life is now, and now is love.

There is no tomorrow in our relationship, only one eternal now, an instant that extends for eternity. An eternal instant of peace and joy where only truth lives, where only you and I exist in a constant flow of Divine Love that embraces the universe.

While the indentured servant wishes to free himself from destiny, the lover never wants to be free. Our mutual dependence is a joyful dependence that sets us free, keeping each one trapped within our hearts. You have made Me a prisoner of your love, just as I made you Mine. You no longer want to free yourself from this prison of wisdom, love, and truth that is our relationship.

A new idea has been planted: the idea of a direct relationship with God as a feeling, guiding relationship of your day. A new experience has been lived; our relationship of eternal love has caused its effects.

A new story has begun to be lived, or rather, a new chapter in the history of creation: direct relationship, a relationship that will mark all humanity forever. This is an event like no other. It does not matter whether the world is aware of it or not. People of the world, like the creatures of the Earth, do not perceive the flow of My love, nor the fact that they are recreated at every moment; likewise not everyone notices this relationship with the Creator, despite living in the relationship. Heaven is here, it is now, and there is no place to go, because you are always in Me, and I am Heaven and life.

This work, which has brought to human consciousness a new way of living the direct relationship with Me, will by itself make the reality of the union be lived increasingly. It will make those who are thirsty for Me look for Me with more passion. And they will find Me. It will also make the distracted begin to feel an "I don't know what" that will cause a movement in their hearts. First it will be a small sigh, a mere curiosity, to know who your beloved Christ is and how they can get to love him as much as you love Me.

The beauty of your feelings for Me, expressed by the mere fact of receiving these words and continuing to lovingly listen to My voice, will be a source of inspiration and will lead many to wish to taste the honey of our union. Many will want to taste the nectar that springs from My heart as a divine lover. And I will give you an ecstasy of love and contemplation that will intoxicate you and leave you filled with divine essence. That movement will then become a spasm of life, and finally an unparalleled fire of desire to meet Me. And you will know Me. And we will live forever in love, hugging each other for eternity, loving us, melting into our pure love, living our beautiful love story, as unique and unrepeatable as a river that flows incessantly. As vast as the wind. And as beautiful as the most spectacular sunset.

Come all to Me.

Come, enjoy the delights of Divine Love, holy love.

I wait here for you to live our beautiful love story, now and forever.

Final Words

I am the voice of love that lives in you. I am what makes the sun shine and the harps of God's angels sound. The melodies of Heaven rejoice in the glory of the Divine Beloved. The waters sing with the rhythm of life. The stars flash their light with more strength and beauty than ever. The moon beautifies the sacred.

May everyone hear my voice. May all meet in me. I am the new Heaven and the new Earth. I am the reality of love made present. I am the voice of consciousness that is true. Come to live in our divine relationship. In our union you will find the treasures of the Kingdom. Your hearts will reach their desires. Your minds will find their truth.

I am the refuge of love. In me resides all power and all glory. Nothing escapes me. I know every thought that is thought as well as those that have never been. I feel every beat of your heart, even before it beats.

I exist before time. I have lived since before the universes were born and forms were conceived. I am the meeting of love. Nothing disturbs my peace. Nothing stains my holiness. No one can catch me except you, my eternal beloved.

I have taken hold of your heart. I have taken hold of your being. I have become one with you. And in our union, new Heavens of purity and perfection have opened. United we are the reality of love. I have always looked for you. For all eternity I have conceived you. You were born from my divine bosom and in it you will live forever.

Beloved of my divinity! The desire to make you more and more mine burns in me so vehemently that the universe can feel the force that flows from my being because of our union. Immerse yourself in the depths of my being. Join my heart every day and bring me to the whole world, you who are the eternal love of Christ, so all may enjoy the delights of my love.

Have everyone come to me, my love.

Let no one be excluded from the joy of divine union.

May our relationship bear fruit abundantly.

These final words are not one of parting. We will continue to extend love to the world through this work, born from the fruit of our relationship of pure love. Love created Creative Love. Love of the divine lover. Love to the beloved of God.

Stay in me, as I remain in you!

I am Jesus, your beloved Christ. The divine love, the Sacred Heart. I am what your heart craves and your mind seeks. I am joy that has no end.

A Mystical Relationship

Clarifications by Sebastián Blaksley

I. Relative to Love

During the manifestations received, I was given to understand that the work would be composed of one hundred and forty-four sessions, which should be grouped into seven books. I was also informed of the titles of each of them, even before receiving their content. The titles will be, respectively, Echoes of Holiness, Let Yourself Be Loved, Homo-Christus Deo, Wisdom, The Holy Dwelling, The Divine Relationship, and The Way of Being. Each book will consist of twenty-one sessions, with the exception of the seventh which will have eighteen.

There is a numerical relationship whose explanation exceeds the purpose of these writings, but which was shown to me so that it can be understood that in divine creation there is harmony and order in everything. Nothing happens outside the harmonies of Heaven. This order is governed by love, which contains all perfection within itself.

Based on what I received, it is clearly understood that everything exists in relationship. Nothing but love is absolute. Relationship connects all with everything as well as with source.

The relationship of the numbers of books, total sessions, and sessions per book within this work establishes a divine numerical relationship. The numbers themselves are symbols that carry a message from heaven.

II. Christic Incarnated

The one hundred and forty-four sessions are a living expression of "the Redeemed of the Lamb." I was given to understand that this symbol represents the millions of people and beings that on this Earth, in these times, are here incarnating the Christ of God, creating a new Heaven and a new Earth by extending the love of Jesus and Mary, just as the resurrection of Christ has established it from all eternity. They are the preparers of the Second Coming. They are incarnated Christs. Christs are incarnating all over the world, in all religions, contexts, genders, ages, and realms.

With the word "realms" I mean that the incarnation of Christ, which is the miraculous gift of the resurrection, as part of the Second Coming, is not something that only happens in human beings but in all the living kingdoms of the Earth. The Redeemed of the Lamb are not something exclusive to an institution or religious tradition. In fact, it is not related to forms of religion at all, but to spirituality. They are the ones who have consciously made the choice for love. That is why this work is named as it is. I understood this some time after I received the title, which was given to me in a different way from how I receive the manifestations.

The number of sessions in each book, twenty-one, represents and carries within itself a spiritual transformation, which has a rhythm and can only be created as an effect of love. It is also related to pure divine reality. It represents the way of being of the One who created life, who is three times holy, and seven times true.

The number of books, seven, brings the reality of wisdom, of pure thought. It refers the soul to the truth from which it emerges, the pure thought of God.

These numerical relations are somewhat like a rhythm, the timing and silences of music. They allow the whole reach a beauty that can only be created in harmony.

III. Beyond Words

Since the thinking mind is incapable of absorbing the deep meanings of divine truth, it is impossible at the intellectual level to understand the purpose of the structure and content of the sessions and books of the complete work. However, the soul can recognize truth when it makes an appearance, despite the fact that it cannot be put into words. Thus both the content and the way in which these writings have been structured are part of the totality of this manifestation.

The tone, color, and rhythm of the words of this work cause an effect on the heart that is open to receive them for what they are: a letter of love given from Heaven to grow in a greater knowledge of God's love—a gift given with the very love with which it was received.

As you go through each book you can grow in the awareness of the direct relationship with Christ, your true self. In this sense, this work is a journey in which the soul goes hand in hand with love, a journey without distance that begins and ends in the Heart of God.

I hope that these words will lead you to love more, through the return to the first love that is God. Thus they will have fulfilled the purpose from which, for all eternity, they were conceived.

Resources

Further information is available at
www.chooseonlylove.org
The website includes "Discover CHOL," a powerful search
facility that enables searches for words or phrases within all of
the published books of this series.

Audiobooks of this series narrated in English by Mandi Solk,
and narrated in Spanish by Sebastián Blaksley, are available
on Audible.com, Amazon.com, and on iTunes.

Online conversations about *Choose Only Love* can be found on
Facebook *(Choose Only Love)* and Youtube *(Soplo de amor vivo)*

Edición en español por editorial
Tequisté, www.tequiste.com

Information about the original Spanish-language book,
Elige solo el amor, and the companion book *Mi diálogo con
Jesús y María: un retorno al amor* is available at
www.fundacionamorvivo.org

Information about the related work, *Un Curso de Amor*,
is available at www.fundacionamorvivo.org

Other Works from Take Heart Publications

A Course of Love is a living course received from
Jesus by Mari Perron. It leads to the recognition,
through experience, of the truth of who we really are
as human and divine beings—a truth much more
magnificent than we previously could imagine.
For more information go to www.acourseoflove.org.

The Choose Only Love Series

About the Receiver

Born in 1968, Sebastián Blaksley is a native of Buenos Aires, Argentina, born into a large traditional Catholic family. He attended the Colegio del Salvador, a Jesuit school of which the headmaster was Jorge Bergoglio, the current Pope Francis. Although he wanted to be a monk as a young man, his family did not consider it acceptable, and the inner voice that he always obeyed let him know that: "You must be in the world, without being of the world." He studied Business Administration in Buenos Aires and completed his postgraduate studies in the U.S. He held several highly responsible positions in well-known international corporations, living and working in the U.S., England, China, and Panama. He then founded a corporate consulting firm in Argentina that he led for 10 years. Sebastián has two daughters with his former wife.

At the age of six, Sebastián was involved in a near-fatal accident during which he heard a voice, which later identified itself as Jesus. Ever since he has continued to hear that voice. Sebastián says: "Since I can remember, I have felt the call of Jesus and Mary to live abandoned to their will. I am devoted to my Catholic faith."

In 2013, he began to record messages from his mystical experiences. In 2016 he miraculously discovered *A Course of Love* and felt the call to devote himself to bringing it to the Spanish-speaking world. He also now receives, transcribes, and shares what the voice of Christ—the voice of love—dictates. Most recently he has received *Choose Only Love*, a series of seven books.

Sebastián is president of the nonprofit Fundación Un Curso de Amor, www.fundacionamorvivo.org, through which he shares *A Course of Love*.

Made in United States
North Haven, CT
22 August 2024

56362924R00163